THE
LIVELY POLL

A Tale of the North Sea

R. M. BALLANTYNE

The Lively Poll

R. M. Ballantyne

© 1st World Library, 2009
PO Box 2211
Fairfield, IA 52556
www.1stworldlibrary.com
First Edition

LCCN: 2009923517

Softcover ISBN: 978-1-4218-8878-1
Hardcover ISBN: 978-1-4218-8977-1
eBook ISBN: 978-1-4218-8779-1

Purchase *"The Lively Poll"*
as a traditional bound book at:
www.1stWorldLibrary.com/purchase.asp?ISBN=978-1-4218-8878-1

1st World Library is a literary, educational organization
dedicated to:

- Creating a free internet library of downloadable ebooks

- Hosting writing competitions and offering book
publishing scholarships.

Interested in more 1st World Library books?
contact: literacy@1stworldlibrary.com
Check us out at: www.1stworldlibrary.com

1ˢᵗ World Library Literary Society

Giving Back to the World

"If you want to work on the core problem, it's early school literacy."

- James Barksdale, former CEO of Netscape

"No skill is more crucial to the future of a child, or to a democratic and prosperous society, than literacy."

- Los Angeles Times

"Literacy... means far more than learning how to read and write... The aim is to transmit... knowledge and promote social participation."

- UNESCO

"Literacy is not a luxury, it is a right and a responsibility. If our world is to meet the challenges of the twenty-first century we must harness the energy and creativity of all our citizens."

- President Bill Clinton

"Parents should be encouraged to read to their children, and teachers should be equipped with all available techniques for teaching literacy, so the varying needs and capacities of individual kids can be taken into account."

- Hugh Mackay

CHAPTER ONE

THE FLEET

Manx Bradley was an admiral—"admiral of the fleet"—though it must be admitted that his personal appearance did not suggest a position so exalted.

With rough pilot coat and sou'-wester, scarred and tarred hands, easy, rolling gait, and boots from heel to hip, with inch-thick soles, like those of a dramatic buccaneer, he bore as little resemblance to the popular idea of a lace-coated, brass-buttoned, cock-hatted admiral as a sea-urchin bears to a cockle-shell. Nevertheless Manx was a real admiral—as real as Nelson, and much harder worked.

His fleet of nearly two hundred fishing-smacks lay bobbing about one fine autumn evening on the North Sea. The vessels cruised round each other, out and in, hither and thither, in all positions, now on this tack, now on that, bowsprits pointing north, south, east, and west, as if without purpose, or engaged in a nautical game of "touch." Nevertheless all eyes were bent earnestly on the admiral's vessel, for it was literally the "flagship," being distinguishable only by a small flag attached to its fore stay.

The fleet was hovering, awaiting orders from the admiral.

A fine smart "fishing breeze" was blowing. The setting sun sparkled on the wave-crests; thin fleecy clouds streaked the sky; everything gave promise of a satisfactory night, and a good haul of fish in the morning.

With the quiet air of an amiable despot Manx nodded his venerable head. Up went the signal, and in a few minutes the fleet was reduced to order. Every smack swept round into position, and, bending over on the same tack, they all rushed like a shoal of startled minnows, away in the same direction—the direction signalled by the admiral. Another signal from our venerable despot sent between one and two hundred trawl-nets down to the bottom of the sea, nets that were strong enough to haul up tons of fish, and rocks, and wreckage, and rubbish, with fifty-feet beams, like young masts, with iron enough in bands and chains to sink them, and so arranged that the beams were raised a few feet off the ground, thus keeping the mouths of the great nets open, while cables many fathoms in length held the gears to their respective vessels.

So the North Sea Fishermen began the night's work—the *Nancy*, the *Coquette*, the *Rattler*, the *Truant*, the *Faith*, the *Playfellow*, the *Cherub*, and all the rest of them. Of course, although the breeze was fresh, they went along slowly, because of the ponderous tails that they had to draw.

Do you ask, reader, why all this order? why this despotic admiral, and all this unity of action? why not "every man for himself"? Let me reply by asking you to think for a moment.

Wind blowing in one direction, perhaps you are aware, does not necessarily imply vessels sailing in the same direction. With variation of courses possible, nearly two

R. M. Ballantyne

hundred tails out astern, and no unity of action, there would arise the certainty of varied and striking incident. The *Nancy* would go crashing into the bows of the *Coquette*, the bowsprit of the *Rallier* would stir up the cabin of the *Truant*, the tail of the *Faith* would get entangled with that of the *Cherub*, and both might hook on to the tail of the *Playfellow*; in short, the awful result would be wreck and wretchedness on the North Sea, howling despair in the markets of Columbia and Billingsgate, and no fish for breakfast in the great metropolis. There is reason for most things—specially good reason for the laws that regulate the fisheries of the North Sea, the fleets of which are over twelve in number, and the floating population over twelve thousand men and boys.

For several hours this shoal of vessels, with full sails and twinkling lights, like a moving city on the deep, continued to tug and plunge along over the "banks" of the German ocean, to the satisfaction of the fishermen, and the surprise no doubt of the fish. About midnight the admiral again signalled, by rocket and flares, "Haul up," and immediately, with capstan, bar, and steam, the obedient crews began to coil in their tails.

It is not our intention to trouble the reader with a minute account of this process or the grand result, but, turning to a particular smack, we solicit attention to that. She is much like the others in size and rig. Her name is the *Lively Poll*. Stephen Lockley is her skipper, as fine a young fisherman as one could wish to see—tall, handsome, free, hearty, and powerful. But indeed all deep-sea fishermen possess the last quality. They would be useless if not physically strong. Many a Samson and Hercules is to be found in the North Sea fleets. "No better nursery or training-school in time of war," they say. That may be true, but it is pleasanter to think of them as a training-school for times of peace.

The night was very dark. Black clouds overspread the sky, so that no light save the dim rays of a lantern cheered the men as they went tramp, tramp, round the capstan, slowly coiling in the trawl-warp. Sheets of spray sometimes burst over the side and drenched them, but they cared nothing for that, being pretty well protected by oilskins, sou'-westers, and sea-boots. Straining and striving, sometimes gaining an inch or two, sometimes a yard or so, while the smack plunged and kicked, the contest seemed like a doubtful one between *vis inertiae* and the human will. Two hours and a half it lasted, until the great trawl-beam came to the surface, and was got up on the vessel's side, after which these indomitable men proceeded to claw up the huge net with their fingers, straining and heaving with might and main.

"Yo, ho!" cried the skipper, "heave her in, boys!"

"Hoy!" growled Peter Jay, the mate, giving a tug that should have torn the net to pieces—but didn't!

"Looks like as if we'd got hold of a lump o' wreck," gasped Bob Lumsden, the smack's boy, who was also the smack's cook.

"No, no, Lumpy," remarked David Duffy, who was no respecter of names or persons, "it ain't a wreck, it's a mermaid. I've bin told they weigh over six ton when young. Look out when she comes aboard—she'll bite."

"I do believe it's old Neptune himself," said Jim Freeman, another of the "hands." "There's his head; an' something like his pitchfork."

R. M. Ballantyne

"It does feel heavier than I ever knowed it afore," remarked Fred Martin.

"That's all along of your bein' ill, Fred," said the mate.

"It may be so," returned Martin, "for I do feel queer, an' a'most as weak as a baby. Come heave away!"

It was indeed a huge mass of wreck entangled with seaweed which had rendered the net so heavy on that occasion, but there was also a satisfactory mass of fish in the "cod-end," or bag, at the extremity of the net, for, when, by the aid of the winch, this cod-end was finally got inboard, and the cord fastening the bottom of it was untied, fish of all kinds gushed over the wet decks in a living cataract.

There were a few expressions of satisfaction from the men, but not much conversation, for heavy work had still to be done—done, too, in the dark. Turbot, sole, cod, skate, and all the other treasures of the deep, had to be then and there gutted, cleaned, and packed in square boxes called "trunks," so as to be ready for the steam-carrier next morning. The net also had to be cleared and let down for another catch before daybreak.

Now it is just possible that it may never have occurred to the reader to consider how difficult, not to say dangerous, must be the operation of gutting, cleaning, and packing fish on a dark night with a smack dancing a North Sea hornpipe under one's feet. Among the dangers are two which merit notice. The one is the fisherman's liability, while working among the "ruck," to run a sharp fish-bone into his hand, the other to gash himself with his knife while attempting to operate on the tail of a skate. Either accident may be slight or it may be severe.

A sudden exclamation from one of the men while employed in this cleaning and packing work told that something had happened.

"There goes Martin," growled Joe Stubley; "you can always tell when it's him, 'cause he don't curse an' swear."

Stubley—or Stubby, as his mates called him—did not intend this for a compliment by any means, though it may sound like one. Being an irreligious as well as a stupid man, he held that all who professed religion were hypocritical and silly. Manliness, in poor Jo's mind, consisted of swagger, quiet insolence, cool cursing, and general godlessness. With the exception of Fred Martin, the rest of the crew of the *Lively Poll* resembled him in his irreligion, but they were very different in character,— Lockley, the skipper being genial; Peter Jay, the mate, very appreciative of humour, though quiet and sedate; Duffy, jovial and funny; Freeman, kindly, though reckless; and Bob, the boy-cook, easy-going both as to mind and morals. They all liked Martin, however, in spite of his religion, for he practised much and preached little.

"What's wrong?" asked Lockley, who stood at the tiller looking out for lights ahead.

"Only a bone into my left hand," replied Martin, going on with his somewhat dirty labours.

"Well that it's no worse, boy," observed Freeman, "for we've got no medicine-chest to fly to like that lucky Short-Blue fleet."

"That's true, Jim," responded Martin; "I wish we had a Gospel smack with our fleet, for our souls need repairing as well as our bodies."

"There you go," growled Stubley, flinging down a just finished fish with a flap of indignation. "A feller can't mention the name o' them mission craft without rousin' you up to some o' your hypocritical chaff. For my part, if it wasn't for the medicine-chest and the mittens, I think we'd be better by a long way without Gospel ships, as ye call 'em. Why, what good 'ave they done the Short-Blues? I'm sure *we* doesn't want churches, or prayin', or psalm-singin' or book—"

"Speak for yourself, Jo," interrupted Puffy.

"Although your head may be as thick as a three-inch plank, through which nothin' a'most can pass either from books or anything else, you mustn't think we've bin all built on the same lines. I likes a good book myself, an', though I don't care about prayin' or psalm-singin', seein' I don't understand 'em, I say 'good luck' to the mission smacks, if it was for nothin' else than the books, an' doctor stuff, an' mitts what the shoregoin' ladies—bless their hearts!—is so fond o' sendin' to us."

"Ay, an the cheap baccy, too, that they say they're a-goin' to send to us," added Freeman.

"P'r'aps they'll send us cheap grog at last," said Puffy, with a laugh.

"They'll hardly do that," remarked Martin; "for it's to try an' keep us from goin' for our baccy to the *copers* that they've started this new plan."

"I wish 'em success," said Lockley, in a serious tone. And there was good ground for that wish, for our genial and handsome skipper was peculiarly weak on the point of strong drink, that being to him a powerful, almost irresistible, temptation.

When the fish-cleaning and packing were completed, the men went below to snatch a few hours' repose. Wet, weary, and sleepy, but with a large stock of reserve strength in them, they retired to the little cabin, in which they could scarcely stand up without bumping their heads, and could hardly turn round without hitting their elbows on something or other. Kicking off their long boots, and throwing aside oilskin coats and sou'-westers, they tumbled into their narrow "bunks" and fell asleep almost without winking.

There was one among them, however, who did not sleep long that night. Fred Martin was soon awakened by the pain of his wound, which had begun to inflame, and by a feeling of giddiness and intense uneasiness with which he had been troubled for several days past.

Turning out at last, he sat down in front of the little iron stove that served to cook food as well as to warm the cabin, and, gazing into the embers, began to meditate on his strangely uncomfortable sensations.

"Hallo, Martin, anything wrong?" asked the mate, who descended at that moment to relight his pipe.

"I believe there is, mate. I never felt like this afore. I've fowt against it till I can hardly stand. I feel as if I was goin' to knock under altogether. This hand, too, seems gittin' bad. I do think my blood must be poisoned, or somethin' o' that sort. You know I don't easily give in, but when a feller feels as if little red-hot wires was twistin' about inside of him, an' sees things goin' round as if he was drunk, why—"

"Why, it's time to think of goin' home," interrupted Jay, with a laugh. "But let's have a look at you, Fred. Well, there does seem to be some o' your riggin' slack. Have you ever had the measles?"

"Not as I knows of."

"Looks like it," said the mate, lighting his pipe. "P'r'aps it'll be as well to send you into dock to refit. You'd better turn in again, anyhow, for a snooze would do you good."

Fred Martin acted on this advice, while Jay returned to the deck; but it was evident that the snooze was not to be had, for he continued to turn and toss uneasily, and to wonder what was wrong with him, as strong healthy men are rather apt to do when suddenly seized with sickness.

At grey dawn the admiral signalled again. The order was to haul up the nets, which had been scraping the bottom of the sea since midnight, and the whole fleet set to work without delay.

Martin turned out with the rest, and tried to defy sickness for a time, but it would not do. The strong man was obliged to succumb to a stronger than he—not, however, until he had assisted as best as he could in hauling up the trawl.

This second haul of the gear of the *Lively Poll* illustrated one of those mishaps, to which all deep-sea trawlers are liable, and which are of frequent occurrence. A piece of wreck or a lost anchor, or something, had caught the net, and torn it badly, so that when it reached the surface all the fish had escaped.

"A night's work for nothing!" exclaimed Stephen Lockley,

with an oath.

"*Might* have been worse," suggested Martin.

By that time it was broad daylight, and as they had no fish to pack, the crew busied themselves in removing the torn net from the beam, and fitting on a new one. At the same time the crews of the other smacks secured their various and varied hauls, cleaned, packed, and got ready for delivery.

The smoke of the steam-carrier was seen on the horizon early in the forenoon, and all the vessels of the fleet made for her, as chickens make for their mother in times of danger.

We may not pause here to describe the picturesque con-fusion that ensued—the arriving, congregating, tacking, crossing, and re-crossing of smacks; the launching of little boats, and loading them with "trunks;" the concentration of these round the steamer like minnows round a whale; the shipping of the cargo, and the tremendous hurry and energy displayed in the desire to do it quickly, and get the fish fresh to market. Suffice it to say that in less than four hours the steamer was loaded, and Fred Martin, fever-stricken and with a highly inflamed hand and arm, started on a thirty-six hours' voyage to London.

Then the fleet sheered off and fell into order, the admiral issued his instructions, and away they all went again to continue the hard, unvarying round of hauling and toiling and moiling, in heat and cold, wet and dry, with nothing to lighten the life or cheer the heart save a game at "crib" or "all fives," or a visit to the *coper*, that terrible curse of the North Sea.

R. M. Ballantyne

CHAPTER TWO

ACCIDENTS AFLOAT AND INCIDENTS ASHORE

Now, although it is an undoubted fact that the skippers of the North Sea trawling smacks are first-rate seamen, it is an equally certain fact that strong drink can render them unfit for duty. One of the skippers was, if we may say so, unmanned by drink at the time the fleet sheered off from the steam-carrier, as stated in the last chapter. He was named Georgie Fox—better known in the fleet as Groggy Fox.

Unfortunately for himself as well as others, Skipper Fox had paid a visit to one of the *copers* the day before for the purpose of laying in a stock of tobacco, which was sold by the skipper of the floating grog-shop at 1 shilling 6 pence a pound. Of course Fox had been treated to a glass of fiery spirits, and had thereafter been induced to purchase a quantity of the same. He had continued to tipple until night, when he retired in a fuddled state to rest. On rising he tippled again, and went on tippling till his fish were put on board the steamer. Then he took the helm of his vessel, and stood with legs very wide apart, an owlish gaze in his eyes, and a look of amazing solemnity on his visage.

When a fleet sheers off from a steam-carrier after delivery of cargo, the sea around is usually very much crowded with vessels, and as these cross and re-cross or run past or alongside of each other before finally settling into the appointed course, there is a good deal of hearty recognition—shouting, questioning, tossing up of arms, and expressions of goodwill—among friends. Several men hailed and saluted Fox as his smack, the *Cormorant*, went by, but he took no notice except with an idiotic wink of both eyes.

"He's bin to the *coper*," remarked Puffy, as the *Cormorant* crossed the bow of the *Lively Poll*. "I say, Lumpy, come here," he added, as Bob Lumsden came on deck. "Have 'ee got any o' that coffee left?"

"No, not a drop. I gave the last o't to Fred Martin just as he was goin' away."

"Poor Fred!" said Puffy. "He's in for suthin' stiff, I doubt, measles or mulligrumps, if not wuss."

"A great pity," remarked Peter Jay, who stood at the helm, "that Martin couldn't hold out a week longer when our turn comes round to run for Yarmouth."

"It's well we got him shipped off to-day," said Lockley. "That hand of his would have made him useless before another day was out. It's a long time for a man in his state to be without help, that run up to Lun'on. Port your helm a bit, Jay. Is it the *Cormorant* that's yawin' about there in that fashion?"

"Ay, it's the *Cormorant*," replied Jay. "I seed her just now a'most run foul o' the *Butterfly*."

"She'll be foul of us. Hi! Look out!" cried Lockley, becoming excited, as he saw the *Cormorant* change her course suddenly, without apparent reason, and bear straight down upon his vessel.

There was, indeed, no reason for the strange movements of the smack in question, except that there was at the helm a man who had rendered his reason incapable of action. With dull, fishy eyes, that stared idiotically at nothing, his hand on the tiller, and his mind asleep, Georgie Fox stood on the deck of the *Cormorant* steering.

"Starboard a bit, Jay," said Lockley, with an anxious look, "she'll barely clear us."

As he spoke, Fox moved his helm slightly. It changed the course of his vessel only a little, but that little sufficed to send the cutwater of the *Cormorant* straight into the port bows of the *Lively Poll* with a tremendous crash, for a smart breeze was blowing at the time. The bulwarks were cut down to the deck, and, as the *Cormorant* recoiled and again surged ahead, the bowsprit was carried away, and part of the topmast brought down.

Deep and fierce was the growl that burst from Lockley's lips at this disaster, but that did not mend matters. The result was that the *Lively Poll* had to quit the fleet a week before her time of eight weeks afloat was up, and run to Yarmouth for repairs. Next day, however, it fell calm, and several days elapsed before she finally made her port.

Meanwhile Fred Martin reached London, with his feverish complaint greatly aggravated, and his undressed wound much worse. In London he was detained some hours by his employers, and then sent on to Yarmouth, which he reached late in the afternoon, and ultimately in a state of great suffering and exhaustion, made his way to Gorleston, where his mother lived.

With his mind in a species of wild whirl, and acute pains darting through his wounded hand and arm, he wended his way slowly along the road that led to his mother's house. Perhaps we should style it her attic, for she could claim only part of the house in which she dwelt. From a quaint gable window of this abode she had a view of the sea over the houses in front.

Part of Fred's route lay along the banks of the Yare, not far from its mouth. At a spot where there were many old anchors and cables, old and new trawl-beams, and sundry other seafaring rusty and tarry objects, the young fisherman met a pretty young girl, who stopped suddenly, and, with her large blue eyes expressing unspeakable surprise, exclaimed, "Fred!"

The youth sprang forward, seized the girl with his uninjured hand, and exclaimed, "Isa!" as he drew her towards him.

"Fred—not here. Behave!" said Isa, holding up a warning finger.

Fred consented to behave—with a promise, however, that he would make up for it at a more fitting time and place.

"But what is the matter!" asked Isa, with an anxious look, laying her pretty little hands on the youth's arm.

Yes, you need not smile, reader; it is not a perquisite of ladies to have pretty little hands. Isa's hands were brown, no doubt, like her cheeks, owing to exposure and sunshine, and they were somewhat roughened by honest toil;

R. M. Ballantyne

but they were small and well-shaped, with taper fingers, and their touch was very tender as she clasped them on her lover's arm.

"Nothing serious," replied the youth lightly; "only an accident with a fish-bone, but it has got to be pretty bad for want of attention; an' besides I'm out o' sorts somehow. No physic, you see, or doctors in our fleet, like the lucky dogs of the Short-Blue. I've been knocked up more or less for some weeks past, so they sent me home to be looked after. But I won't need either physic or doctor now."

"No? why not?" asked the girl, with a simple look.

"Cause the sight o' your sweet face does away with the need of either."

"Don't talk nonsense, Fred."

"If that's nonsense," returned the fisherman, "you'll never hear me talk sense again as long as I live. But how about mother, Isa? Is she well!"

"Quite well. I have just left her puzzling herself over a letter from abroad that's so ill-written that it would bother a schoolmaster to read it. I tried to read it, but couldn't. You're a good scholar, Fred, so you have come just in time to help her. But won't she be surprised to see you!"

Thus conversing, and walking rather slowly, the pair made their way to the attic of Mrs Martin, where the unexpected sight of her son threw the patient woman into a great flutter of surprise and pleasure. We use the word "patient" advisedly, for Mrs Martin was one of those wholesome-minded creatures who, having to battle vigorously for the bare necessaries of life in the face of many adverse circumstances, carry on the war with a degree of hearty, sweet-tempered resolution which might put to shame many who are better off in every way. Mrs Martin was a widow and a washerwoman, and had a ne'er-do-well brother, a fisherman, who frequently "sponged" upon her. She also had a mother to support and attend upon, as well as a "bad leg" to endure. True, the attendance on her mother was to the good woman a source of great joy. It constituted one of the few sunbeams of her existence, but it was not on that account the less costly, for the old woman could do nothing whatever to increase the income of the widow's household—she could not, indeed, move a step without assistance. Her sole occupation was to sit in the attic window and gaze over the sands upon the sea, smiling hopefully, yet with a touch of sadness in the smile; mouthing her toothless gums, and muttering now and then as if to herself, "He'll come soon now." Her usual attitude was that of one who listens expectantly.

Thirty years before Granny Martin had stood at the same attic window, an elderly woman even then, looking out upon the raging sea, and muttering anxiously the same words, "He'll come soon now." But her husband never came. He was lost at sea. As years flew by, and time as well as grief weakened her mind, the old woman seemed to forget the flight of time, and spent the greater part of every day in the attic window, evidently on the look-out for some one who was to come "soon." When at last she was unable to walk alone, and had to be half carried to her seat in the attic window by her strong and loving daughter, the sadness seemed to pass away, and her cheery spirit revived under the impression, apparently, that the coming could not be delayed much longer. To every one Granny was condescendingly kind, especially

R. M. Ballantyne

to her grandchild Fred, of whom she was very fond.

Only at intervals was the old woman's cheerfulness disturbed, and that was during the occasional visits of her ne'er-do-well son Dick, for he was generally drunk or "half-seas-over" when he came. Granny never mentioned his name when he was absent, and for a long time Mrs Martin supposed that she tried to forget him, but her opinion changed on this point one night when she overheard her mother praying with intense earnestness and in affectionate terms that her dear Dick might yet be saved. Still, however much or frequently Granny's thoughts might at any time be distracted from their main channel, they invariably returned thereto with the cheerful assurance that "*he* would soon come now."

"You're ill, my boy," said Mrs Martin, after the first greetings were over.

"Right you are, mother," said the worn-out man, sitting down with a weary sigh. "I've done my best to fight it down, but it won't do."

"You must have the doctor, Fred."

"I've had the doctor already, mother. I parted with Isa Wentworth at the bottom o' the stair, an' she will do me more good than dozens o' doctors or gallons o' physic."

But Fred was wrong.

Not long afterwards the *Lively Poll* arrived in port, and Stephen Lockley hastened to announce his arrival to his wife.

Now it was the experience of Martha Lockley that if, on

his regular return to land for his eight days' holiday, after his eight weeks' spell afloat, her handsome and genial husband went straight home, she was wont to have a happy meeting; but if by any chance Stephen first paid a visit to the Blue Boar public-house, she was pretty sure to have a miserable meeting, and a more or less wretched time of it thereafter. A conversation that Stephen had recently had with Fred Martin having made an impression on him—deeper than he chose to admit even to himself—he had made up his mind to go straight home this time.

"I'll be down by daybreak to see about them repairs," he said to Peter Jay, as they left the *Lively Poll* together, "and I'll go round by your old friend, Widow Mooney's, and tell her to expect you some time to-night."

Now Peter Jay was a single man, and lodged with Widow Mooney when on shore. It was not, however, pure consideration for his mate or the widow that influenced Lockley, but his love for the widow's little invalid child, Eve, for whose benefit that North Sea skipper had, in the kindness of his heart, made a special collection of deep-sea shells, with some shreds of bright bunting.

Little Eve Mooney, thin, wasted, and sad, sat propped up with dirty pillows, in a dirty bed, in a dirtier room, close to a broken and paper-patched window that opened upon a coal-yard with a prospect rubbish-heap beyond.

"Oh, I'm *so* glad it's you!" cried Eve, with flushed cheeks and sparkling eyes, as the fisherman entered.

"Yes, Eve, my pretty. I'm back sooner than I expected—and look what I've brought you. I haven't forgot you."

Joy beamed in the lustrous eyes and on every feature of

R. M. Ballantyne

the thin face as the sick child surveyed the treasures of the deep that Lockley spread on her ragged counterpane.

"How good—how kind of you, Stephen!" exclaimed Eve.

"Kind!" repeated the skipper; "nothing of the sort, Eve. To please you pleases me, so it's only selfishness. But where's your mother?"

"Drunk," said the child simply, and without the most remote intention of injuring her parent's character. Indeed, that was past injury. "She's in there."

The child pointed to a closet, in which Stephen found on the floor a heap of unwomanly rags. He was unable to arouse the poor creature, who slumbered heavily beneath them. Eve said she had been there for many hours.

"She forgot to give me my breakfast before she went in, and I'm too weak to rise and get it for myself," whimpered Eve, "and I'm *so* hungry! And I got such a fright, too, for a man came in this morning about daylight and broke open the chest where mother keeps her money and took something away. I suppose he thought I was asleep, for I was too frightened to move, but I could see him all the time. Please will you hand me the loaf before you go? It's in that cupboard."

We need scarcely add that Lockley did all that the sick child asked him to do—and more. Then, after watching her till the meal was finished, he rose.

"I'll go now, my pretty," he said, "and don't you be afeared. I'll soon send some one to look after you. Good-bye."

Stephen Lockley was unusually thoughtful as he left Widow Mooney's hut that day, and he took particular care to give the Blue Boar a wide berth on his way home.

R. M. Ballantyne

CHAPTER THREE

THE SKIPPER ASHORE

Right glad was Mrs Lockley to find that her husband had passed the Blue Boar without going in on his way home, and although she did not say so, she could not feel sorry for the accident to the *Lively Poll*, which had sent him ashore a week before his proper time.

Martha Lockley was a pretty young woman, and the proud mother of a magnificent baby, which was bordering on that age when a child begins to have some sort of regard for its own father, and to claim much of his attention.

"Matty," said Stephen to his wife, as he jolted his daughter into a state of wild delight on his knee, "Tottie is becoming very like you. She's got the same pretty little turned-up nose, an' the same huge grey eyes with the wicked twinkle in 'em about the corners."

"Don't talk nonsense, Stephen, but tell me about this robbery."

"I know nothin' about it more than I've told ye, Matty. Eve didn't know the man, and her description of him is confused—she was frightened, poor thing! But I promised to send some one to look after her at once, for her drunken mother isn't fit to take care of herself, let alone the sick child. Who can I send, think 'ee?"

Mrs Lockley pursed her little mouth, knitted her brows, and gazed thoughtfully at the baby, who, taking the look as personal, made a face at her. Finally she suggested Isabella Wentworth.

"And where is she to be found?" asked the skipper.

"At the Martins', no doubt," replied Mrs Lockley, with a meaning look. "She's been there pretty much ever since poor Fred Martin came home, looking after old granny, for Mrs Martin's time is taken up wi' nursing her son. They say he's pretty bad."

"Then I'll go an' see about it at once," said Stephen, rising, and setting Tottie down.

He found Isa quite willing to go to Eve, though Mrs Mooney had stormed at her and shut the door in her face on the occasion of her last visit.

"But you mustn't try to see Fred," she added. "The doctor says he must be kep' quiet and see no one."

"All right," returned the skipper; "I'll wait till he's out o' quarantine. Good day; I'll go and tell Eve that you're coming."

On his way to Mrs Mooney's hut Stephen Lockley had again to pass the Blue Boar. This time he did not give it "a wide berth." There were two roads to the hut, and the shorter was that which passed the public-house. Trusting

R. M. Ballantyne

to the strength of his own resolution, he chose that road. When close to the blue monster, whose creaking sign drew so many to the verge of destruction, and plunged so many over into the gulf, he was met by Skipper Ned Bryce, a sociable, reckless sort of man, of whom he was rather fond. Bryce was skipper of the *Fairy*, an iron smack, which was known in the fleet as the Ironclad.

"Hullo! Stephen. *You* here?"

"Ay, a week before my time, Ned. That lubber Groggy Fox ran into me, cut down my bulwarks, and carried away my bowsprit an' some o' my top-hamper."

"Come along—have a glass, an' let's hear all about it," said Bryce, seizing his friend's arm; but Lockley held back.

"No, Ned," he said; "I'm on another tack just now."

"What! not hoisted the blue ribbon, eh!"

"No," returned Lockley, with a laugh. "I've no need to do that."

"You haven't lost faith in your own power o' self-denial surely?"

"No, nor that either, but—but—"

"Come now, none o' your 'buts.' Come along; my mate Dick Martin is in here, an' he's the best o' company."

"Dick Martin in there!" repeated Lockley, on whom a sudden thought flashed. "Is he one o' your hands?"

"In course he is. Left the Grimsby fleet a-purpose to j'ine me. Rather surly he is at times, no doubt, but a good fellow at bottom, and great company. You should hear him sing. Come."

"Oh, I know him well enough by hearsay, but never met him yet."

Whether it was the urgency of his friend, or a desire to meet with Dick Martin, that shook our skipper's wavering resolution we cannot tell, but he went into the Blue Boar, and took a glass for good-fellowship. Being a man of strong passions and excitable nerves, this glass produced in him a desire for a second, and that for a third, until he forgot his intended visit to Eve, his promises to his wife, and his stern resolves not to submit any longer to the tyranny of drink. Still, the memory of Mrs Mooney's conduct, and of the advice of his friend Fred Martin, had the effect of restraining him to some extent, so that he was only what his comrades would have called a little screwed when they had become rather drunk.

There are many stages of drunkenness. One of them is the confidential stage. When Dick Martin had reached this stage, he turned with a superhumanly solemn countenance to Bryce and winked.

"If—if you th-think," said Bryce thickly, "th-that winkin' suits you, you're mistaken."

"Look 'ere," said Dick, drawing a letter from his pocket with a maudlin leer, and holding it up before his comrade, who frowned at it, and then shook his head—as well he might, for, besides being very illegibly written, the letter was presented to him upside down.

R. M. Ballantyne

After holding it before him in silence long enough to impress him with the importance of the document, Dick Martin explained that it was a letter which he had stolen from his sister's house, because it contained "something to his advantage."

"See here," he said, holding the letter close to his own eyes, still upside down, and evidently reading from memory: "'If Mr Frederick Martin will c-call at this office any day next week between 10 an' 12, h-he will 'ear suthin' to his ad-advantage. Bounce and Brag, s'licitors.' There!"

"But *you* ain't Fred Martin," said Bryce, with a look of supreme contempt, for he had arrived at the quarrelsome stage of drunkenness.

"Right you are," said Martin; "but I'm his uncle. Same name c-'cause his mother m-married her c-cousin; and there ain't much difference 'tween Dick and Fred—four letters, both of 'em—so if I goes wi' the letter, an' says, 'I'm Fred Martin,' w'y, they'll hand over the blunt, or the jewels, or wotiver it is, to me—d'ee see?"

"No, I don't see," returned Bryce so irritatingly that his comrade left the confidential stage astern, and requested to know, with an affable air, when Bryce lost his eyesight.

"When I first saw *you*, and thought you worth your salt," shouted Bryce, as he brought his fist heavily down on the table.

Both men were passionate. They sprang up, grappled each other by the throat, and fell on the floor. In doing so they let the letter fall. It fluttered to the ground, and Lockley, quietly picking it up, put it in his pocket.

"You'd better look after them," said Lockley to the landlord, as he paid his reckoning, and went out.

In a few minutes he stood in Widow Mooney's hut, and found Isa Wentworth already there.

"I'm glad you sent me here," said the girl, "for Mrs Mooney has gone out—"

She stopped and looked earnestly in Lockley's face. "You've been to the Blue Boar," she said in a serious tone.

"Yes, lass, I have," admitted the skipper, but without a touch of resentment. "I did not mean to go, but it's as well that I did, for I've rescued a letter from Dick Martin which seems to be of some importance, an' he says he stole it from his sister's house."

He handed the letter to the girl, who at once recognised it as the epistle over which she and Mrs Martin had puzzled so much, and which had finally been deciphered for them by Dick Martin.

"He must have made up his mind to pretend that he is Fred," said Isa, "and so get anything that was intended for him."

"You're a sharp girl, Isa; you've hit the nail fair on the head, for I heard him in his drunken swagger boast of his intention to do that very thing. Now, will you take in hand, lass, to give the letter back to Mrs Martin, and explain how you came by it?"

Of course Isa agreed to do so, and Lockley, turning to Eve, said he would tell her a story before going home.

R. M. Ballantyne

The handsome young skipper was in the habit of entertaining the sick child with marvellous tales of the sea during his frequent visits, for he was exceedingly fond of her, and never failed to call during his periodical returns to land. His love was well bestowed, for poor Eve, besides being of an affectionate nature, was an extremely imaginative child, and delighted in everything marvellous or romantic. On this occasion, however, he was interrupted at the commencement of his tale by the entrance of his own ship's cook, the boy Bob Lumsden, *alias* Lumpy.

"Hullo, Lumpy, what brings you here?" asked the skipper.

But the boy made no answer. He was evidently taken aback at the unexpected sight of the sick child, and the skipper had to repeat his question in a sterner tone. Even then Lumpy did not look at his commander, but, addressing the child, said—

"Beg parding, miss; I wouldn't have come in if I'd knowed you was in bed, but—"

"Oh, never mind," interrupted Eve, with a little smile, on seeing that he hesitated; "my friends never see me except in bed. Indeed I live in bed; but you must not think I'm lazy. It's only that my back's bad. Come in and sit down."

"Well, boy," demanded the skipper again, "were you sent here to find *me*?"

"Yes, sir," said Lumpy, with his eyes still fixed on the earnest little face of Eve. "Mister Jay sent me to say he wants to speak to you about the heel o' the noo bowsprit."

"Tell him I'll be aboard in half an hour."

"I didn't know before," said Eve, "that bowsprits have heels."

At this Lumpy opened his large mouth, nearly shut his small eyes, and was on the point of giving vent to a rousing laugh, when his commander half rose and seized hold of a wooden stool. The boy shut his mouth instantly, and fled into the street, where he let go the laugh which had been thus suddenly checked.

"Well, she *is* a rum 'un!" he said to himself, as he rolled in a nautical fashion down to the wharf where the *Lively Poll* was undergoing repairs.

"I think he's a funny boy, that," said Eve, as the skipper stooped to kiss her.

"Yes, he *is* a funny dog. Good-bye, my pretty one."

"Stay," said Eve solemnly, as she laid her delicate little hand on the huge brown fist of the fisherman; "you've often told me stories, Stephen; I want to tell one to you to-night. You need not sit down; it's a very, very short one."

But the skipper did sit down, and listened with a look of interest and expectation as the child began—

"There was once a great, strong, brave man, who was very kind to everybody, most of all to little children. One day he was walking near a river, when a great, fearful, ugly beast, came out of the wood, and seized the man with its terrible teeth. It was far stronger than the dear, good man, and it threw him down, and held him down, till—till it killed him."

She stopped, and tears filled her soft eyes at the scene she

R. M. Ballantyne

had conjured up.

"Do you know," she asked in a deeper tone, "what sort of awful beast it was?"

"No; what was it?"

"A Blue Boar," said the child, pressing the strong hand which she detained.

Lockley's eyes fell for a moment before Eve's earnest gaze, and a flush deepened the colour of his bronzed countenance. Then he sprang suddenly up and kissed Eve's forehead.

"Thank you, my pretty one, for your story, but it an't just correct, for the man is not quite killed *yet* and, please God, he'll escape."

As he spoke the door of the hut received a severe blow, as if some heavy body had fallen against it. When Isa opened it, a dirty bundle of rags and humanity rolled upon the floor. It was Eve's mother!

Lifting her up in his strong arms, Lockley carried her into the closet which opened off the outer room, and laid her tenderly on a mattress which lay on the floor. Then, without a word, he left the hut and went home.

It is scarcely necessary to add that he took the longer road on that occasion, and gave a very wide berth indeed to the Blue Boar.

CHAPTER FOUR

HARDSHIPS ON THE SEA

Fly with us now, good reader, once more out among the breeze-ruffled billows of the North Sea.

It was blowing a fine, fresh, frosty fishing breeze from the nor'-west on a certain afternoon in December. The Admiral—Manx Bradley—was guiding his fleet over that part of the German Ocean which is described on the deep-sea fisherman's chart as the Swarte, or Black Bank. The trawls were down, and the men were taking it easy—at least, as easy as was compatible with slush-covered decks, a bitter blast, and a rolling sea. If we had the power of extending and intensifying your vision, reader, so as to enable you to take the whole fleet in at one stupendous glance, and penetrate planks as if they were plate glass, we might, perhaps, convince you that in this multitude of deep-sea homes there was carried on that night a wonderful amount of vigorous action, good and bad—largely, if not chiefly bad—under very peculiar circumstances, and that there was room for improvement everywhere.

Strong and bulky and wiry men were gambling and drinking, and singing and swearing; story-telling and

R. M. Ballantyne

fighting, and skylarking and sleeping. The last may be classed appropriately under the head of action, if we take into account the sonorous doings of throats and noses. As if to render the round of human procedure complete, there was at least one man—perhaps more—praying.

Yes, Manx Bradley, the admiral, was praying. And his prayer was remarkably brief, as well as earnest. Its request was that God would send help to the souls of the men whose home was the North Sea. For upwards of thirty years Manx and a few like-minded men had persistently put up that petition. During the last few years of that time they had mingled thanksgiving with the prayer, for a gracious answer was being given. God had put it into the heart of the present Director of the Mission to Deep-Sea Fishermen to inaugurate a system of evangelisation among the heretofore neglected thousands of men and boys who toil upon the North Sea from January to December. Mission or Gospel smacks were purchased, manned by Christian skippers and crews, and sent out to the various fleets, to fish with them during the week, and supply them with medicine for body and soul, with lending libraries of wholesome Christian literature, and with other elevating influences, not least among which was a floating church or meeting-house on Sundays.

But up to the time we write of, Manx Bradley had only been able to rejoice in the blessing as sent to others. It had not yet reached his own fleet, the twelve or thirteen hundred men and boys of which were still left in their original condition of semi-savagery, and exposure to the baleful influences of that pest of the North Sea—the *coper*.

"You see, Jacob Jones," said the admiral to the only one of his "hands" who sympathised with him in regard to religion, "if it warn't for the baccy, them accursed *copers* wouldn't be able to keep sich a hold of us. Why, bless you, there's many a young feller in this fleet as don't want no grog—especially the vile, fiery stuff the *copers* sell 'em; but when the Dutchmen offers the baccy so cheap as 1 shilling 6 pence a pound, the boys are only too glad to go aboard and git it. Then the Dutchmen, being un-common sly dogs, gives 'em a glass o' their vile brandy for good-fellowship by way of, an' that flies to their heads, an' makes 'em want more—d'ee see? An' so they go on till many of 'em becomes regular topers—that's where it is, Jacob."

"Why don't the mission smacks sell baccy too?" asked Jacob, stamping his feet on the slushy deck to warm them, and beating his right hand on the tiller for the same purpose.

"You're a knowing fellow," returned the admiral, with a short laugh; "why, that's just what they've bin considerin' about at the Head Office—leastwise, so I'm told; an' if they manage to supply the fleets wi' baccy at 1 shilling a pound, which is 6 pence less than the Dutchmen do, they'll soon knock the *copers* off the North Sea altogether. But the worst of it is that *we* won't git no benefit o' that move till a mission smack is sent to our own fleet, an' to the half-dozen other fleets that have got none."

At this point the state of the weather claiming his attention, the admiral went forward, and left Jacob Jones, who was a new hand in the fleet, to his meditations.

One of the smacks which drew her trawl that night over the Swarte Bank not far from the admiral was the *Lively Poll*—repaired, and rendered as fit for service as ever.

Not far from her sailed the *Cherub*, and the *Cormorant*, and that inappropriately named *Fairy*, the "ironclad."

In the little box of the *Lively Poll*—which out of courtesy we shall style the cabin—Jim Freeman and David Duffy were playing cards, and Stephen Lockley was smoking. Joe Stubby was drinking, smoking, and grumbling at the weather; Hawkson, a new hand shipped in place of Fred Martin, was looking on. The rest were on deck.

"What's the use o' grumblin', Stub?" said Hawkson, lifting a live coal with his fingers to light his pipe.

"Don't 'Stub' me," said Stubley in an angry tone.

"Would you rather like me to stab you?" asked Hawkson, with a good-humoured glance, as he puffed at his pipe.

"I'd rather you clapped a stopper on your jaw."

"Ah—so's you might have all the jawin' to yourself?" retorted Hawkson.

Whatever reply Joe Stubley meant to make was interrupted by Jim Freeman exclaiming with an oath that he had lost again, and would play no more. He flung down the cards recklessly, and David Duffy gathered them up, with the twinkling smile of a good-natured victor.

"Come, let's have a yarn," cried Freeman, filling his pipe, with the intention of soothing his vanquished spirit.

"Who'll spin it?" asked Duffy, sitting down, and preparing to add to the fumes of the place. "Come, Stub, you tape it off; it'll be better occupation than growlin' at the poor weather, what's never done you no harm yet though there's no sayin' what it may do if you go on as you've bin doin', growlin' an' aggravatin' it."

"I never spin yarns," said Stubley.

"But you tell stories sometimes, don't you?" asked Hawkson.

"No, never."

"Oh! that's a story anyhow," cried Freeman.

"Come, I'll spin ye one," said the skipper, in that hearty tone which had an irresistible tendency to put hearers in good humour, and sometimes even raised the growling spirit of Joe Stubley into something like amiability.

"What sort o' yarn d'ee want, boys?" he asked, stirring the fire in the small stove that warmed the little cabin; "shall it be comical or sentimental?"

"Let's have a true ghost story," cried Puffy.

"No, no," said Freeman, "a hanecdote—that's what I'm fondest of— suthin' short an' sweet, as the little boy said to the stick o' liquorice."

"Tell us," said Stubley, "how it was you come to be saved the night the *Saucy Jane* went down."

"Ah! lads," said Lockley, with a look and a tone of gravity, "there's no fun in that story. It was too terrible and only by a miracle, or rather—as poor Fred Martin said at the time—by God's mercy, I was saved."

R. M. Ballantyne

"Was Fred there at the time!" asked Duffy.

"Ay, an' very near lost he was too. I thought he would never get over it."

"Poor chap!" said Freeman; "he don't seem to be likely to git over this arm. It's been a long time bad now."

"Oh, he'll get over that," returned Lockley; "in fact, it's a'most quite well now, I'm told, an' he's pretty strong again—though the fever did pull him down a bit. It's not that, it's money, that's keepin' him from goin' afloat again."

"How's that?" asked Puffy.

"This is how it was. He got a letter which axed him to call on a lawyer in Lun'on, who told him an old friend of his father had made a lot o' tin out in Austeralia, an' he died, an' left some hundreds o' pounds—I don't know how many—to his mother."

"Humph! that's just like him, the hypercrit," growled Joe Stubley; "no sooner comes a breeze o' good luck than off he goes, too big and mighty for his old business. He was always preachin' that money was the root of all evil, an' now he's found it out for a fact."

"No, Fred never said that 'money was the root of all evil,' you thick-head," returned Duffy; "he said it was the *love* of money. Put that in your pipe and smoke it—or rather, in your glass an' drink it, for that's the way to get it clearer in your fuddled brain."

"Hold on, boys; you're forgettin' my yarn," interposed Lockley at this point, for he saw that Stubley was beginning to lose temper. "Well, you must know it was about six years ago—I was little more than a big lad at the time, on board the *Saucy Jane*, Black Thomson bein' the skipper. You've heard o' Black Thomson, that used to be so cruel to the boys when he was in liquor, which was pretty nigh always, for it would be hard to say when he wasn't in liquor? He tried it on wi' me when I first went aboard, but I was too—well, well, poor fellow, I'll say nothin' against him, for he's gone now."

"Fred Martin was there at the time, an' it was wonderful what a hold Fred had over that old sinner. None of us could understand it, for Fred never tried to curry favour with him, an' once or twice I heard him when he thought nobody was near, givin' advice to Black Thomson about drink, in his quiet earnest way, that made me expect to see the skipper knock him down. But he didn't. He took it well—only he didn't take his advice, but kep' on drinkin' harder than ever. Whenever a *coper* came in sight at that time Thomson was sure to have the boat over the side an' pay him a visit.

"Well, about this time o' the year there came one night a most tremendous gale, wi' thick snow, from the nor'ard. It was all we could do to make out anything twenty fathom ahead of us. The skipper he was lyin' drunk down below. We was close reefed and laying to with the foresail a-weather, lookin' out anxiously, for, the fleet bein' all round and the snow thick, our chances o' runnin' foul o' suthin' was considerable. When we took in the last reef we could hardly stand to do it, the wind was so strong—an' wasn't it freezin', too! Sharp enough a'most to freeze the nose off your face.

"About midnight the wind began to shift about and came in squalls so hard that we could scarcely stand, so we took

R. M. Ballantyne

in the jib and mizzen, and lay to under the foresail. Of course the hatchways was battened down and tarpaulined, for the seas that came aboard was fearful. When I was standin' there, expectin' every moment that we should founder, a sea came and swept Fred Martin overboard. Of course we could do nothing for him—we could only hold on for our lives; but the very next sea washed him right on deck again. He never gave a cry, but I heard him say 'Praise the Lord!' in his own quiet way when he laid hold o' the starboard shrouds beside me.

"Just then another sea came aboard an' a'most knocked the senses out o' me. At the same moment I heard a tremendous crash, an' saw the mast go by the board. What happened after that I never could rightly understand. I grabbed at something—it felt like a bit of plank—and held on tight, you may be sure, for the cold had by that time got such a hold o' me that I knew if I let go I would go down like a stone. I had scarce got hold of it when I was seized round the neck by something behind me an' a'most choked.

"I couldn't look round to see what it was, but I could see a great black object coming straight at me. I knew well it was a smack, an' gave a roar that might have done credit to a young walrus. The smack seemed to sheer off a bit, an' I heard a voice shout, 'Starboard hard! I've got him,' an' I got a blow on my cocoanut that well-nigh cracked it. At the same time a boat-hook caught my coat collar an' held on. In a few seconds more I was hauled on board of the *Cherub* by Manx Bradley, an' the feller that was clingin' to my neck like a young lobster was Fred Martin. The *Saucy Jane* went to the bottom that night."

"An' Black Thomson—did he go down with her?" asked Duffy.

"Ay, that was the end of him and all the rest of the crew. The fleet lost five smacks that night."

"Admiral's a-signallin', sir," said one of the watch on deck, putting his head down the hatch at that moment.

Lockley went on deck at once. Another moment, and the shout came down—"Haul! Haul all!"

Instantly the sleepers turned out all through the fleet. Oiled frocks, sou'-westers, and long boots were drawn on, and the men hurried on the decks to face the sleet-laden blast and man the capstan bars, with the prospect before them of many hours of hard toil—heaving and hauling and fish-cleaning and packing with benumbed fingers— before the dreary winter night should give place to the grey light of a scarcely less dreary day.

R. M. Ballantyne

CHAPTER FIVE

THE TEMPTER'S VICTORY

"I wouldn't mind the frost or snow, or anything else," growled Joe Stubley, pausing in the midst of his labours among the fish, "if it warn't for them sea-blisters. Just look at that, Jim," he added, turning up the hard sleeve of his oiled coat, and exposing a wrist which the feeble rays of the lantern showed to be badly excoriated and inflamed.

"Ay, it's an ugly bracelet, an' I've got one myself just begun on my left wrist," remarked Jim Freeman, also suspending labour for a moment to glance at his mate's wound. "If our fleet had a mission ship, like some o' the other fleets, we'd not only have worsted mitts for our wrists, but worsted helmets for our heads an' necks—to say nothin' of lotions, pills an' plasters."

"If they'd only fetch us them things an' let alone tracts, Bibles, an' religion," returned Stubley, "I'd have no objection to 'em, but what's the use o' religion to a drinkin', swearin', gamblin' lot like us?"

"It's quite clear that your notions about religion are muddled," said David Duffy, with a short laugh. "Why, what's the use o' physic to a sick man, Stubs?"

"To make him wuss," replied Stubs promptly.

"You might as well argify with a lobster as with Joe Stubs," said Bob Lumsden, who, although burdened with the cares of the cooking department, worked with the men at cleaning and packing.

"What does a boy like you know about lobsters, 'cept to cook 'em?" growled Stubley. "You mind your pots an' pans. That's all your brains are fit for—if you have brains at all. Leave argification to men."

"That's just what I was advisin' Duffy to do, an' not waste his breath on the likes o' you," retorted the boy, with a grin.

The conversation was stopped at this point by the skipper ordering the men to shake out a reef, as the wind was moderating. By the time this was accomplished daybreak was lighting up the eastern horizon, and ere long the pale grey of the cold sea began to warm up a little under the influence of the not yet visible sun.

"Goin' to be fine," said Lockley, as he scanned the horizon with his glass.

"Looks like it," replied the mate.

Remarks were few and brief at that early hour, for the men, being pretty well fagged, preferred to carry on their monotonous work in silence.

As morning advanced the fleet was clearly seen in all directions and at all distances around, holding on the same course as the *Lively Poll*. Gradually the breeze moderated, and before noon the day had turned out bright and sunny, with only a few thin clouds floating in the wintry sky. By that time the fish-boxes, or trunks, were all packed, and the men availed themselves of the brief period of idleness pending the arrival of the steam-carrier from Billingsgate to eat a hearty breakfast.

This meal, it may be remarked, was a moveable feast, depending very much on the duties in hand and the arrival of the steamer. To get the fish ready and shipped for market is always regarded as his first and all-important duty by the deep-sea trawler, who, until it is performed, will not condescend to give attention to such secondary matters as food and repose. These are usually taken when opportunity serves. Pipes and recreation, in the form of games at cards, draughts, dominoes, and yarns, are also snatched at intervals between the periods of severe toil. Nevertheless, there are times when the fisherman's experience is very different. When prolonged calms render fishing impossible, then time hangs heavily on his hands, and—in regard to the fleet of which we write and all those similarly circumstanced—the only recreations available are sleeping, drinking, gambling, and yarn-spinning. True, such calms do not frequently occur in winter, but they sometimes do, and one of them prevailed on the afternoon of the particular winter's day, of which we treat.

After the departure of the carrier that day, the wind fell so much that the admiral deemed it advisable not to put down the nets. Before long the light air died away alto-gether, and the fleet was left floating idly, in picturesque groups and with flapping sails, on the glassy sea.

Among the groups thus scattered about, there was one

smack which had quietly joined the fleet when the men were busy transhipping or "ferrying" the fish to the steam-carrier. Its rig was so similar to that of the other smacks that a stranger might have taken it for one of the fleet but the fishermen knew better. It was that enemy of souls, that floating grog-shop, that pirate of the North Sea, the *coper*.

"Good luck to 'ee," muttered Joe Stubley, whose sharp, because sympathetic, eye was first to observe the vessel.

"It's bad luck to *you* anyhow," remarked Bob the cook, who chanced to pass at the moment.

"Mind your own business, Lumpy, an' none o' your sauce, if you don't want a rope's-endin'," retorted the man.

"Ain't I just mindin' my own business? Why, wot is sauce but part of a cook's business?" returned the boy.

"I *won't* go to her," thought Stephen Lockley, who over-heard the conversation, and in whose breast a struggle had been going on, for he also had seen the *coper*, and, his case-bottle having run dry, he was severely tempted to have it replenished.

"Would it not be as well, skipper, to go aboard o' the *coper*, as she's so near at hand!" said the mate, coming aft at the moment.

"Well, no, Peter; I think it would be as well to drop the *coper* altogether. The abominable stuff the Dutchmen sell us is enough to poison a shark. You know I'm not a teetotaller, but if I'm to be killed at all, I'd rather be killed by good spirits than bad."

"Right you are," replied Jay, "but, you see, a lot of us are hard up for baccy, and—"

"Of course, of course; the men must have baccy," interrupted the skipper, "an' we don't need to buy their vile brandy unless we like. Yes, get the boat out, Jay, an' we'll go."

Stephen Lockley was not the first man who has deceived himself as to his motives. Tobacco was his excuse for visiting the floating den of temptation, but a craving for strong drink was his real motive. This craving had been created imperceptibly, and had been growing by degrees for some years past, twining its octopus arms tighter and tighter round his being, until the strong and hearty young fisherman was slowly but surely becoming an abject slave, though he had fancied himself heretofore as free as the breezes that whistled round his vessel. Now, for the first time, Lockley began to have uncomfortable suspicions about himself. Being naturally bold and candid, he turned sharply round, and, as it were, faced *himself* with the stern question, "Stephen, are you sure that it's baccy that tempts you aboard of the *coper*? Are you clear that schnapps has nothing to do with it?"

It is one of the characteristics of the slavery to which we refer, that although strong-minded and resolute men put pointed questions of this sort to themselves not unfrequently, they very seldom return answers to them. Their once vigorous spirits, it would seem, are still capable of an occasional heave and struggle—a sort of flash in the pan—but that is all. The influence of the depraved appetite immediately weighs them down, and they relapse into willing submission to the bondage. Lockley had not returned an answer to his own question when the mate reported that the boat was ready. Without a word he jumped into her, but kept thinking to himself,

"We'll only get baccy, an' I'll leave the *coper* before the lads can do themselves any harm. I'll not taste a drop myself—not a single drop o' their vile stuff."

The Dutch skipper of the *coper* had a round fat face and person, and a jovial, hearty manner. He received the visitors with an air of open-handed hospitality which seemed to indicate that nothing was further from his thoughts than gain.

"We've come for baccy," said Lockley, as he leaped over the bulwarks and shook hands, "I s'pose you've plenty of that?"

"Ya," the Dutchman had "plenty tabac—ver sheep too, an' mit sooch a goot vlavour!"

He was what the Yankees would call a 'cute fellow, that Dutchman. Observing the emphasis with which Lockley mentioned tobacco, he understood at once that the skipper did not want his men to drink, and laid his snares accordingly.

"Com'," he said, in a confidential tone, taking hold of Lockley's arm, "com' b'low, an' you shall zee de tabac, an' smell him yourself."

Our skipper accepted the invitation, went below, and was soon busy commenting on the weed, which, as the Dutchman truly pointed out, was "*so* sheep as well as goot." But another smell in that cabin overpowered that of the tobacco. It was the smell of Hollands, or some sort of spirit, which soon aroused the craving that had gained such power over the fisherman.

"Have some schnapps!" said the Dutch skipper, suddenly

R. M. Ballantyne

producing a case-bottle as square as himself, and pouring out a glass.

"No, thank 'ee," said Stephen firmly.

"No!" exclaimed the other, with well-feigned surprise. "You not drink?"

"Oh yes, I drink," replied Lockley, with a laugh, "but not to-day."

"I not ask you to buy," rejoined the tempter, holding the spirits a little nearer to his victim's nose. "Joost take von leetle glass for goot vellowship."

It seemed rude to decline a proposal so liberally made, and with such a smiling countenance. Lockley took the glass, drank it off and went hurriedly on deck, followed by the Dutchman, with the case-bottle in one hand and the glass in the other. Of course the men had no objection to be treated. They had a small glass all round.

"That's the stuff for my money!" cried Stubley, smacking his lips. "I say, old chap, let's have a bottle of it. None o' your thimblefuls for me. I like a good swig when I'm at it."

"You'd better wait till we get aboard, Joe, before you begin," suggested Lockley, who was well aware of Joe's tendencies.

Joe admitted the propriety of this advice, but said he would treat his mates to one glass before starting, by "way o' wetting their whistles."

"Ya, joost von glass vor vet deir vistles," echoed the

Dutchman, with a wink and a look which produced a roar of laughter. The glass was accepted by all, including Lockley, who had been quite demoralised by the first glass.

The victory was gained by the tempter for that time at least. The fishermen who went for baccy, remained for schnapps, and some of them were very soon more than half drunk. It was a fierce, maddening kind of spirit, which produced its powerful effects quickly.

The skipper of the *Lively Poll* kept himself better in hand than his men, but, being very sociable in disposition, and finding the Dutchman a humorous and chatty fellow, he saw no reason to hurry them away. Besides, his vessel was close alongside, and nothing could be done in the fishing way during the dead calm that prevailed.

While he and his men were engaged in a lively conversation about nothing in particular—though they were as earnest over it as if the fate of empires depended on their judgment—the Dutch skipper rose to welcome another boat's crew, which approached on the other side of the *coper*. So eager and fuddled were the disputants of the *Lively Poll* that they did not at first observe the newcomers.

It was the *Fairy's* boat, with Dick Martin in charge.

"Hallo, Dick, mein boy; gif me your vlipper."

A sign from Martin induced the Dutchman to lean over the side and speak in lower tones.

"Let's have a keg of it," said Dick, with a mysterious look. "Ned Bryce sent me for a good supply, an' here's *fish* to pay for it."

The fish—which of course belonged to the owner of the *Fairy*, not to Ned Bryce—were quickly passed up, and a keg of spirits passed down. Then the Dutchman asked if Dick or his men wanted tabac or schnapps for themselves.

"I vill take jersey, or vish, or sail, or boots, or vat you please in exchange. Com' aboard, anyhow, an' have von leetle glass."

Dick and his men having thus smartly transacted their chief business, leaped on deck, made fast their painter, let the boat drop astern, and were soon smoking and drinking amicably with the crew of the *Lively Poll*. Not long afterwards they were quarrelling. Then Dick Martin, who was apt to become pugnacious over his liquor, asserted stoutly that something or other "was." Joe Stubley swore that it "*was not*," whereupon Dick Martin planted his fist on Joe Stubley's nose and laid its growly owner flat on the deck.

Starting up, Joe was about to retaliate, when Lockley, seizing him by the neck thrust him over the side into the boat, and ordered his more or less drunken crew to follow. They did so with a bad grace, but the order was given in a tone which they well understood must not be disobeyed.

As they pushed off, Stubley staggered and fell into the sea. Another moment and he would have been beyond all human aid, but Lockley caught a glimpse of his shaggy black head as it sank. Plunging his long right arm down, and holding on to the boat with his left, he caught the drowning man by the hair. Strong and willing arms helped, and Stubley was hauled inboard—restored to life, opportunity, and hope—and flung into the bottom of the boat.

The oars were shipped, and they pulled for the *Lively Poll*. As they rode away they saw that other boats were proceeding towards the *coper*. The men in them were all anxious to buy baccy. No mention was made of drink. Oh dear no! They cared nothing for that, though, of course, they had no sort of objection to accept the wily Dutchman's generous offer of "von leetle glass vor goot vellowship."

R. M. Ballantyne

CHAPTER SIX

THE POWER OF SYMPATHY

One fine afternoon, not long after the visit to the *coper*, Bob Lumsden, *alias* Lumpy, was called from his culinary labours to assist in hauling in the net.

Now it is extremely interesting to note what a wonderful effect the power of loving sympathy can have on a human being. Lumpy was a human being—though some of his mates insisted that he must have been descended from a cod-fish, because his mouth was so large. No doubt it was, and when the boy laughed heartily he was, indeed, apt to remind one of that fish; nevertheless it was a good, well-shaped mouth, though large, with a kindly expression about it, and a set of splendid white teeth inside of it. But, whether human or fishy in his nature, Bob Lumsden had been overwhelmed by a flood of sympathy ever since that memorable day when he had first caught a glimpse of the sweet, pale face of the little invalid Eve Mooney. It was but a brief glimpse, yet it had opened a new sluice in Lumpy's heart, through which the waters of tenderness gushed in a wild torrent.

One of the curious results of this flood was that Bob was always more prompt to the summons to haul up the trawl than he had ever been before, more energetic in clawing the net inboard, and more eager to see and examine the contents of the cod-end. The explanation is simple. He had overheard his skipper say how fond Eve was of shells —especially of those which came from the bottom of the North Sea, and of all sorts of pretty and curious things, wherever they came from.

From that hour Bob Lumpy became a diligent collector of marine curiosities, and the very small particular corner of the vessel which he called his own became ere long quite a museum. They say that sympathy is apt to grow stronger between persons of opposite constitutions. If this be so, perhaps it was his nature—his bold, hearty, gushing, skylarking spirit, his strong rugged frame, his robust health, his carroty hair, his appley cheeks, his eagle nose, his flashing eyes—that drew him so powerfully to the helpless, tender little invalid, with her delicate frame and pale cheeks, straight little nose, bud of a mouth, and timid, though by no means cowardly, spirit.

On another occasion Bob overheard Lockley again talking about Eve. "I'm sorry for the poor thing," he said to Peter Jay, as they paced the deck together; "she's got such a wretched home, an' her mother's such a drunken bru—"

Lockley checked himself, and did not finish the sentence.

"The doctor says," he resumed, "that if Eve had only a bath-chair or suthin' o' that sort, to get wheeled about in the fresh air, she'd very likely get better as she growed older—specially if she had good victuals. You see, small as she is, and young as she looks, she's over fifteen. But even if she had the chair, poor thing! who would wheel it for her? It would be no use unless it was done regular, an' her mother can't do it—or won't."

R. M. Ballantyne

From that hour Bob Lumpy became a miser. He had been a smoker like the rest of the crew, but he gave up "baccy." He used to take an occasional glass of beer or spirits when on shore or on board the *copers*, but he became a total abstainer, much to his own benefit in every way, and as a result he became rich—in an extremely small way.

There was a very small, thin, and dirty, but lively and intelligent boy in Yarmouth, who loved Bob Lumsden better, if possible, than himself. His name was Pat Stiver. The affection was mutual. Bob took this boy into his confidence.

One day, a considerable time after Bob's discovery of Eve, Pat, having nothing to do, sauntered to the end of Gorleston Pier, and there to his inexpressible joy, met his friend. Before he had recovered sufficiently from surprise to utter a word, Bob seized him by the arms, lifted him up, and shook him.

"Take care, Lumpy," cried the boy, "I'm wery tender, like an over-young chicken. You'd better set me down before I comes in pieces."

"Why, Stiver, you're the very man I was thinkin' of," said Lumpy, setting the boy on the edge of the pier, and sitting down beside him.

Stiver looked proud, and felt six inches taller.

"Listen," said Bob, with an earnest look that was apt to captivate his friends; "I want help. Will you do somethin' for me?"

"Anything," replied the boy with emphasis, "from pitch and toss to manslaughter!"

"Well, look here. You know Eve Mooney?"

"Do I know the blessedest angel in all Gorleston? In course I does. Wot of her?"

"She's ill—very ill," said Lumpy.

"You might as well tell me, when it's daytime, that the sun's up," returned Pat.

"Don't be so awful sharp, Stiver, else I'll have to snub you."

"Which you've on'y got to frown, Bob Lumpy, an' the deed's done."

Bob gave a short laugh, and then proceeded to explain matters to his friend: how he had been saving up his wages for some time past to buy a second-hand bath-chair for Eve, because the doctor had said it would do her so much good, especially if backed up with good victuals.

"It's the wittles as bothers me, Stiver," said Bob, regarding his friend with a puzzled expression.

"H'm! well," returned the small boy seriously, "wittles has bothered me too, off an' on, pretty well since I was born, though I'm bound to confess I does get a full blow-out now an'—"

"Hold on, Stiver; you're away on the wrong tack," cried Bob, interrupting. "I don't mean the difficulty o' findin' wittles, but how to get Eve to take 'em."

"Tell her to shut her eyes an' open her mouth, an' then shove 'em in," suggested Pat.

"I'll shove you into the sea if you go on talking balder-dash," said Bob. "Now, look here, you hain't got nothin' to do, have you!"

"If you mean in the way o' my purfession, Bob, you're right. I purfess to do anything, but nobody as yet has axed me to do nothin'. In the ways o' huntin' up wittles, howsever, I've plenty to do. It's hard lines, and yet I ain't extravagant in my expectations. Most coves require three good meals a day, w'ereas I'm content with one. I begins at breakfast, an' I goes on a-eatin' promiskoously all day till arter supper—w'en I can get it."

"Just so, Stiver. Now, I want to engage you profess-sionally. Your dooties will be to hang about Mrs Mooney's, but in an offhand, careless sort o' way, like them superintendent chaps as git five or six hundred a year for doin' nuffin, an' be ready at any time to offer to give Eve a shove in the chair. But first you'll have to take the chair to her, an' say it was sent to her from—"

"Robert Lumsden, Esquire," said Pat, seeing that his friend hesitated.

"Not at all, you little idiot," said Bob sharply. "You mustn't mention my name on no account."

"From a gentleman, then," suggested Pat.

"That might do; but I ain't a gentleman, Stiver, an' I can't allow you to go an' tell lies."

"I'd like to know who is if you ain't," returned the boy indignantly. "Ain't a gentleman a man wot's gentle? An' w'en you was the other day a-spreadin' of them lovely shells, an' crabs, an' sea-goin' kooriosities out on her pocket-hankercher, didn't I *see* that you was gentle?"

"I'll be pretty rough on you, Pat, in a minit, if you don't hold your jaw," interrupted Bob, who, however, did not seem displeased with his friend's definition of a gentleman. "Well, you may say what you like, only be sure you say what's true. An' then you'll have to take some nice things as I'll get for her from time to time w'en I comes ashore. But there'll be difficulties, I doubt, in the way of gettin' her to take wittles w'en she don't know who they comes from."

"Oh, don't you bother your head about that," said Pat. "I'll manage it. I'm used to difficulties. Just you leave it to me, an' it'll be all right."

"Well, I will, Pat; so you'll come round with me to the old furnitur' shop in Yarmouth, an' fetch the chair. I got it awful cheap from the old chap as keeps the shop w'en I told him what it was for. Then you'll bring it out to Eve, an' try to git her to have a ride in it to-day, if you can. I'll see about the wittles arter. Hain't quite worked that out in my mind yet. Now, as to wages. I fear I can't offer you none—"

"I never axed for none," retorted Pat proudly.

"That's true Pat; but I'm not a-goin' to make you slave for nuthin'. I'll just promise you that I'll save all I can o' my wages, an' give you what I can spare. You'll just have to trust me as to that."

"Trust you, Bob!" exclaimed Pat, with enthusiasm, "look here, now; this is how the wind blows. If the Prime Minister o' Rooshia was to come to me in full regimentals an' offer to make me capting o' the Horse Marines to the

Hemperor, I'd say, 'No thankee, I'm engaged,' as the young woman said to the young man she didn't want to marry."

The matter being thus satisfactorily settled, Bob Lumsden and his little friend went off to Yarmouth, intent on carrying out the first part of their plan.

It chanced about the same time that another couple were having a quiet chat together in the neighbourhood of Gorleston Pier. Fred Martin and Isa Wentworth had met by appointment to talk over a subject of peculiar interest to themselves. Let us approach and become eavesdroppers.

"Now, Fred," said Isa, with a good deal of decision in her tone, "I'm not at all satisfied with your explanation. These mysterious and long visits you make to London ought to be accounted for, and as I have agreed to become your wife within the next three or four months, just to please *you*, the least you can do, I think, is to have no secrets from *me*. Besides, you have no idea what the people here and your former shipmates are saying about you."

"Indeed, dear lass, what do they say?"

"Well, they say now you've got well they can't understand why you should go loafing about doin' nothin' or idling your time in London, instead of goin' to sea."

"Idlin' my time!" exclaimed Fred with affected indigation. "How do they know I'm idlin' my time? What if I was studyin' to be a doctor or a parson?"

"Perhaps they'd say that *was* idlin' your time, seein' that you're only a fisherman," returned Isa, looking up in her lover's face with a bright smile. "But tell me, Fred, why should you have any secret from *me*?"

"Because, dear lass, the thing that gives me so much pleasure and hope is not absolutely fixed, and I don't want you to be made anxious. This much I will tell you, however: you know I passed my examination for skipper when I was home last time, and now, through God's goodness, I have been offered the command of a smack. If all goes well, I hope to sail in her next week; then, on my return, I hope to—to take the happiest. Well, well, I'll say no more about that, as we're gettin' near mother's door. But tell me, Isa, has Uncle Martin been worrying mother again when I was away?"

"No. When he found out that you had got the money that was left to her, and had bought an annuity for her with it, he went away, and I've not seen him since."

"That's well. I'm glad of that."

"But am I to hear nothing more about this smack, not even her name?"

"Nothing more just now, Isa. As to her name, it's not yet fixed. But, trust me, you shall know all in good time."

As they had now reached the foot of Mrs Martin's stair, the subject was dropped.

They found the good woman in the act of supplying Granny Martin with a cup of tea. There was obvious improvement in the attic. Sundry little articles of luxury were there which had not been there before.

"You see, my boy," said Mrs Martin to Fred, as they sat

round the social board, "now that the Lord has sent me enough to get along without slavin' as I used—to do, I takes more time to make granny comfortable, an' I've got her a noo chair, and noo specs, which she was much in want of, for the old uns was scratched to that extent you could hardly see through 'em, besides bein' cracked across both eyes. Ain't they much better, dear?"

The old woman, seated in the attic window, turned her head towards the tea-table and nodded benignantly once or twice; but the kind look soon faded into the wonted air of patient contentment, and the old head turned to the sea as the needle turns to the pole, and the soft murmur was heard, "He'll come soon now."

CHAPTER SEVEN

A RESCUE

Never was there a fishing smack more inappropriately named than the *Fairy*,—that unwieldy iron vessel which the fleet, in facetious content, had dubbed the "Ironclad," and which had the honour of being commanded by that free and easy, sociable—almost too sociable—skipper, Ned Bryce.

She was steered by Dick Martin on the day of which we now write. Dick, as he stood at the helm, with stern visage, bloodshot eyes, and dissipated look, was not a pleasant object of contemplation, but as he played a prominent part in the proceedings of that memorable day, we are bound to draw attention to him. Although he had spent a considerable portion of the night with his skipper in testing the quality of some schnapps which they had recently procured from a *coper*, he had retained his physical and mental powers sufficiently for the performance of his duties. Indeed, he was one of those so-called seasoned casks, who are seldom or never completely disabled by drink, although thoroughly enslaved, and he was now quite competent to steer the *Fairy* in safety through the mazes of that complex dance which the deep-sea trawlers usually perform on the arrival of the carrying-steamer.

What Bryce called a chopping and a lumpy sea was running. It was decidedly rough, though the breeze was moderate, so that the smacks all round were alternately presenting sterns and bowsprits to the sky in a violent manner that might have suggested the idea of a rearing and kicking dance. When the carrier steamed up to the Admiral, and lay to beside him, and the smacks drew towards her from all points of the compass, the mazes of the dance became intricate, and the risk of collisions called for careful steering.

Being aware of this, and being himself not quite so steady about the head as he could wish, Skipper Bryce looked at Martin for a few seconds, and then ordered him to go help to launch the boat and get the trunks out, and send Phil Morgan aft.

Phil was not a better seaman than Dick, but he was a more temperate man, therefore clearer brained and more dependable.

Soon the smacks were waltzing and kicking round each other on every possible tack, crossing and re-crossing bows and sterns; sometimes close shaving, out and in, down-the-middle-and-up-again fashion, which, to a landsman, might have been suggestive of the 'bus, cab, and van throng in the neighbourhood of that heart of the world, the Bank of England.

Sounds of hailing and chaffing now began to roll over the North Sea from many stentorian lungs.

"What cheer? what cheer?" cried some in passing.

"Hallo, Tim! how are 'ee, old man! What luck?"

"All right, Jim; on'y six trunks."

"Ha! that's 'cause ye fished up a dead man yesterday."

"Is that you, Ted?"

"Ay, ay, what's left o' me—worse luck. I thought your mother was goin' to keep you at home this trip to mind the babby."

"So she was, boy, but the babby fell into a can o' buttermilk an' got drownded, so I had to come off again, d'ee see?"

"What cheer, Groggy Fox? Have 'ee hoisted the blue ribbon yet?"

"No, Stephen Lockley, I haven't, nor don't mean to, but one o' the fleet seems to have hoisted the blue flag."

Groggy Fox pointed to one of the surrounding vessels as he swept past in the *Cormorant*.

Lockley looked round in haste, and, to his surprise, saw floating among the smaller flags, at a short distance, the great twenty-feet flag of a mission vessel, with the letters MDSF (Mission to Deep-Sea Fishermen) on it, in white on a blue ground.

"She must have lost her reckoning," muttered Lockley, as he tried to catch sight of the vessel to which the flag belonged—which was not easy, owing to the crowd of smacks passing to and fro between it and him.

Just at that moment a hearty cheer was heard to issue from the Admiral's smack, the *Cherub*. At the same time the boat of the *Lively Poll* was launched into the sea, Duffy and Freeman and another hand tumbled into her, and the skipper had to give his undivided attention to the all-important matter of transhipping the fish.

Dozens of boats were by that time bobbing like corks on the heaving sea, all making for the attendant steamer. Other dozens, which had already reached her, were clinging on—the men heaving the fish-boxes aboard,—while yet others were pushing off from the smacks last arrived to join the busy swarm.

Among these was the boat of the *Fairy*, with Dick Martin and two men aboard. It was heavily laden—too heavily for such a sea—for their haul on the previous night had been very successful.

North Sea fishermen are so used to danger that they are apt to despise it. Both Bryce and Martin knew they had too many trunks in the boat, but they thought it a pity to leave five or six behind, and be obliged to make two trips for so small a number, where one might do. Besides, they could be careful. And so they were—very careful; yet despite all their care they shipped a good deal of water, and the skipper stood on the deck of the *Fairy* watching them with some anxiety. Well he might, for so high were the waves that not only his own boat but all the others kept disappearing and re-appearing continually, as they rose on the crests or sank into the hollows.

But Skipper Bryce had eyes for only one boat. He saw it rise to view and disappear steadily, regularly, until it was about half-way to the steamer; then suddenly it failed to rise, and next moment three heads were seen amid the tumultuous waters where the boat should have been.

With a tremendous shout Bryce sprang to the tiller and altered the vessel's course, but, as the wind blew, he knew well it was not in his power to render timely aid. That peculiar cry which tells so unmistakably of deadly disaster was raised from the boats nearest to that which had sunk, and they were rowed towards the drowning men, but the boats were heavy and slow of motion. Already they were too late, for two out of the three men had sunk to rise no more—dragged down by their heavy boots and winter clothing. Only one continued the struggle. It was Dick Martin. He had grasped an oar, and, being able to swim, kept his head up. The intense cold of the sea, however, would soon have relaxed even his iron grip, and he would certainly have perished, had it not been that the recently arrived mission vessel chanced to be a very short distance to windward of him. A slight touch of the helm sent her swiftly to his side. A rope was thrown. Martin caught it. Ready hands and eager hearts were there to grasp and rescue. In another moment he was saved, and the vessel swept on to mingle with the other smacks—for Martin was at first almost insensible, and could not tell to which vessel of the fleet he belonged.

Yes, the bad man was rescued, though no one would have sustained much loss by his death; but in Yarmouth that night there was one woman, who little thought that she was a widow, and several little ones who knew not that they were fatherless. The other man who perished was an unmarried youth, but he left an invalid mother to lifelong mourning over the insatiable greed of the cold North Sea.

Little note was taken of this event in the fleet. It was, in truth, a by no means unusual disaster. If fish are to be found, fair weather or foul, for the tables on land, lives

R. M. Ballantyne

must be risked and lost in the waters of the sea. Loss of life in ferrying the fish being of almost daily occurrence, men unavoidably get used to it, as surgeons do to suffering and soldiers to bloodshed. Besides, on such occasions, in the great turmoil of winds and waves, and crowds of trawlers and shouting, it may be only a small portion of the fleet which is at first aware that disaster has occurred, and even these must not, cannot, turn aside from business at such times to think about the woes of their fellow-men.

Meanwhile Dick Martin had fallen, as the saying is, upon his feet. He was carried into a neatly furnished cabin, put between warm blankets in a comfortable berth, and had a cup of steaming hot coffee urged upon him by a pleasant-voiced sailor, who, while he inquired earnestly as to how he felt, at the same time thanked the Lord fervently that they had been the means of saving his life.

CHAPTER EIGHT

TELLS OF MORE THAN ONE SURPRISE

"Was that your boat that went down?" shouted Groggy Fox of the *Cormorant*, as he sailed past the *Fairy*, after the carrying-steamer had left, and the numerous fishing-smacks were gradually falling into order for another attack on the finny hosts of the sea.

They were almost too far apart for the reply to be heard, and possibly Bryce's state of mind prevented his raising his voice sufficiently, but it was believed that the answer was "Yes."

"Poor fellows!" muttered Fox, who was a man of tender feelings, although apt to feel more for himself than for any one else.

"I think Dick Martin was in the boat," said the mate of the *Cormorant*, who stood beside his skipper. "I saw them when they shoved off, and though it was a longish distance, I could make him out by his size, an' the fur cap he wore."

"Well, the world won't lose much if he's gone," returned Fox; "he was a bad lot."

R. M. Ballantyne

It did not occur to the skipper at that time that he himself was nearly, if not quite, as bad a "lot." But bad men are proverbially blind to their own faults.

"He was a cross-grained fellow," returned the mate, "specially when in liquor, but I never heard no worse of 'im than that."

"Didn't you?" said Fox; "didn't you hear what they said of 'im at Gorleston?—that he tried to do his sister out of a lot o' money as was left her by some cove or other in furrin parts. An' some folk are quite sure that it was him as stole the little savin's o' that poor widdy, Mrs Mooney, though they can't just prove it agin him. Ah, he is a bad lot, an' no mistake. But I may say that o' the whole bilin' o' the Martins. Look at Fred, now."

"Well, wot of him?" asked the mate, in a somewhat gruff tone.

"What of him!" repeated the skipper, "ain't he a hypocrite, with his smooth tongue an' his sly ways, as if butter wouldn't melt in his mouth, an' now—where is he?"

"Well, *where* is he!" demanded the mate, with increasing gruffness.

"Why, in course nobody knows where he is," retorted the skipper; "that's where it is. No sooner does he get a small windfall—leastwise, his mother gets it—than he cuts the trawlers, an' all his old friends without so much as sayin' 'Good-bye,' an' goes off to Lunnon or somewheres, to set up for a gentleman, I suppose."

"I don't believe nothin' o' the sort," returned the mate indignantly. "Fred Martin may be smooth-tongued and shy if you like, but he's no hypercrite—"

"Hallo! there's that mission ship on the lee bow," cried Fox, interrupting his mate, and going over to the lee side of the smack, whence he could see the vessel with the great blue flag clearly. "Port your helm," he added in a deep growl to the man who steered. "I'll give her a wide berth."

"If she was the *coper* you'd steer the other way," remarked the mate, with a laugh.

"In course I would," retorted Fox, "for there I'd find cheap baccy and brandy."

"Ay, bad brandy," said the mate; "but, skipper, you can get baccy cheaper aboard the mission ships now than aboard the *coper*."

"What! at a shillin' a pound?"

"Ay, at a shillin' a pound."

"I don't believe it."

"But it's a fact," returned the mate firmly, "for Simon Brooks, as was in the Short-Blue fleet last week, told me it's a noo regulation— they've started the sale o' baccy in the Gospel ships, just to keep us from going to the *copers*."

"That'll not keep *me* from going to the *copers*," said Groggy Fox, with an oath.

"Nor me," said his mate, with a laugh; "but, skipper, as we are pretty nigh out o' baccy just now, an' as the

R. M. Ballantyne

mission ship is near us, an' the breeze down, I don't see no reason why we shouldn't go aboard an' see whether the reports be true. We go to buy baccy, you know, an' we're not bound to buy everything the shop has to sell! We don't want their religion, an' they can't force it down our throats whether we will or no."

Groggy Fox vented a loud laugh at the bare supposition of such treatment of his throat, admitted that his mate was right, and gave orders to launch the boat. In a few minutes they were rowing over the still heaving but now somewhat calmer sea, for the wind had fallen suddenly, and the smacks lay knocking about at no great distance from each other.

It was evident from the bustle on board many of them, and the launching of boats over their bulwarks, that not a few of the men intended to take advantage of this unexpected visit of a mission vessel. No doubt their motives were various. Probably some went, like the men of the *Cormorant*, merely for baccy; some for medicine; others, perhaps, out of curiosity; while a few, no doubt, went with more or less of desire after the "good tidings," which they were aware had been carried to several of the other fleets that laboured on the same fishing-grounds.

Whatever the reasons, it was evident that a goodly number of men were making for the vessel with the great blue flag. Some had already reached her; more were on their way. The *Cormorant's* boat was among the last to arrive.

"What does MDSF stand for?" asked Skipper Fox, as they drew near.

"Mission to Deep-Sea Fishermen," answered the mate,

whose knowledge on this and other points of the Mission were due to his intercourse with his friend Simon Brooks of the Short-Blue. "But it means more than that," he continued. "When we are close enough to make 'em out, you'll see little letters *above* the MDSF which make the words I've just told you, an' there are little letters *below* the MDSF which make the words Mighty Deliverer, Saviour, Friend."

"Ay! That's a clever dodge," observed Groggy Fox, who, it need hardly be said, was more impressed with the ingenuity of the device than with the grand truth conveyed.

"But I say, mate, they seems to be uncommonly lively aboard of her."

This was obviously the case, for by that time the boat of the *Cormorant* had come so near to the vessel that they could not only perceive the actions of those on board, but could hear their voices. The curiosity of Skipper Fox and his men was greatly roused, for they felt convinced that the mere visit of a passing mission ship did not fully account for the vigorous hand-shakings of those on the deck, and the hearty hailing of newcomers, and the enthusiastic cheers of some at least of the little boats' crews as they pulled alongside.

"Seems to me as if they've all gone mad," remarked Groggy Fox, with a sarcastic grin.

"I would say they was all drunk, or half-seas over," observed the mate, "if it was a *coper*, but in a Gospel ship that's impossible, 'cause they're teetotal, you know. Isn't that the boat o' the Admiral that's pullin' alongside just now, skipper?"

R. M. Ballantyne

"Looks like it, mate. Ay, an' that's Stephen Lockley of the *Lively Poll* close astarn of 'im—an' ain't they kickin' up a rumpus now!"

Fox was right, for when the two little boats referred to ranged alongside of the vessel, and the men scrambled up the side on to her deck, there was an amount of greeting, and hand-shaking, and exclaiming in joyful surprise, which threw all previous exhibitions in that way quite into the shade, and culminated in a mighty cheer, the power of which soft people with shore-going throats and lungs and imaginations cannot hope to emulate or comprehend!

The cheer was mildly repeated with mingled laughter when the crowd on deck turned to observe the arrival of the *Cormorant's* boat.

"Why, it's the skipper o' the *Ironclad*!" exclaimed a voice. "No, it's not. It's the skipper o' the *Cormorant*," cried another.

"What cheer? what cheer, Groggy Fox?" cried a third, as the boat swooped alongside, and several strong arms were extended. "Who'd have looked for *you* here? There ain't no schnapps."

"All right, mates," replied Fox, with an apologetic smile, as he alighted on the deck and looked round; "I've come for *baccy*."

A short laugh greeted this reply, but it was instantly checked, for at the moment Fred Martin stepped forward, grasped the skipper's horny hand, and shook it warmly, as well as powerfully, for Fred was a muscular man, and had fully recovered his strength.

"You've come to the right shop for baccy," he said; "I've got plenty o' that, besides many other things much better. I bid you heartily welcome on board of the *Sunbeam* in the name of the Lord!"

For a few seconds the skipper of the *Cormorant* could not utter a word. He gazed at Fred Martin with his mouth partially, and his eyes wide, open. The thought that he was thus cordially received by the very man whose character he had so lately and so ungenerously traduced had something, perhaps, to do with his silence.

"A-are—are *you* the skipper o' this here wessel!" he stammered.

"Ay, through God's goodness I am."

"A *mission* wessel!" said Fox, his amazement not a whit abated as he looked round.

"Just so, a Gospel ship," answered Fred, giving the skipper another shake of the hand.

"You didn't mistake it for a *coper*, did 'ee?" asked David Duffy, who was one of the visitors.

The laugh which followed this question drowned Groggy Fox's reply.

"And you'll be glad to hear," said Fred, still addressing Fox, "that the *Sunbeam* is a new mission ship, and has been appointed to do service for God in *this* fleet and no other; so you'll always be able to have books and baccy, mitts, helmets, comforters, medicines, and, best of all, Bibles and advice for body and soul, free gratis when you want 'em."

R. M. Ballantyne

"But where's the doctor to give out the medicines," asked Fox, who began to moderate his gaze as he recovered self-possession.

"Well, mate," answered Fred, with a bashful air, "I am doctor as well as skipper. Indeed, I'm parson too—a sort of Jack-of-all-trades! I'm not full fledged of course, but on the principle, I fancy, that 'half a loaf is better than no bread,' I've been sent here after goin' through a short course o' trainin' in surgery—also in divinity; something like city missionaries and Scripture-readers; not that trainin', much or little, would fit any man for the great work unless he had the love of the Master in his heart. But I trust I have that."

"You have, Fred, thank God!" said the Admiral of the fleet.

"And now, Skipper Fox," continued Fred facetiously, "as I'm a sort of doctor, you must allow me to prescribe something for your complaint. Here, boy," he added, hailing one of his crew, "fetch Skipper Fox a draught o' that physic—the brown stuff that you keep in the kettle."

"Ay, ay, sir," answered a youthful voice, and in another minute Pat Stiver forced his way through the crowd, bearing in his hand a large cup or bowl of coffee.

"It's not exactly the tipple I'm used to," said Fox, accepting the cup with a grin, and wisely resolving to make the best of circumstances, all the more readily that he observed other visitors had been, or still were, enjoying the same beverage. "Howsever, it's not to be expected that sick men shall have their physic exactly to their likin', so I thank 'ee all the same, Dr Martin!"

This reply was received with much approval, and the character of Groggy Fox immediately experienced a considerable rise in the estimation of his comrades of the fleet.

Attention was drawn from him just then by the approach of another boat.

"There is some genuine surgeon's work coming to you in that boat, Fred, if I mistake not," remarked Stephen Lockley, as he stood beside his old friend.

"Hasn't that man in the stern got his head tied up?"

"Looks like it."

"By the way, what of your uncle, Dick Martin?" asked the Admiral. "It was you that picked him up, wasn't it?"

This reference to the sad event which had occurred that morning solemnised the fishermen assembled on the *Sunbeam's* deck, and they stood listening with sympathetic expressions as Fred narrated what he had seen of the catastrophe, and told that his uncle was evidently nothing the worse of it, and was lying asleep in the cabin, where everything had been done for his recovery and comfort.

In the boat which soon came alongside was a fisherman who had met with a bad accident some days before. A block tackle from aloft had fallen on his head and cut it severely. His mates had bound it up in rough-and-ready fashion; but the wound had bled freely, and the clotted blood still hung about his hair. Latterly the wound had festered, and gave him agonising pain. His comrades being utterly ignorant as to the proper treatment, could do

R. M. Ballantyne

nothing for him. Indeed, the only effectual thing that could be done was to send the poor man home. This sudden and unexpected appearance of one of the mission ships was therefore hailed as a godsend, for it was well-known that these vessels contained medicines, and it was believed that their skippers were more or less instructed in the healing art. In this belief they were right; for in addition to the well-appointed medicine-chest, each vessel has a skipper who undergoes a certain amount of instruction, and possesses a practical and plain book of directions specially prepared under the supervision of the Board of Trade for the use of captains at sea.

One can imagine, therefore, what a relief it was to this poor wounded man to be taken down into the cabin and have his head at last attended to by one who "knew what he was about." The operation of dressing was watched with the deepest interest and curiosity by the fishermen assembled there, for it was their first experience of the value, even in temporal matters, of a Gospel ship. Their ears were open, too, as well as their eyes, and they listened with much interest to Fred Martin as he tried, after a silent prayer for the Holy Spirit's influence, to turn his first operation to spiritual account in his Master's interest.

"Tell me if I hurt you," he said, observing that his patient winced a little when he was removing the bandage.

"Go on," said the man quietly. "I ain't a babby to mind a touch of pain."

The cabin being too small to hold them all, some of the visitors clustered round the open skylight, and gazed eagerly down, while a few who could not find a point of vantage contented themselves with listening. Even Dick

Martin was an observer at that operation, for, having been roused by the bustle around him, he raised himself on an elbow, and looking down from his berth, could both hear and see.

"There now," said Fred Martin, when at last the bandage was removed and the festering mass laid bare. "Hand the scissors, Pat."

Pat Stiver, who was assistant-surgeon on that occasion, promptly handed his chief the desired instrument, and stood by for further orders.

"I'll soon relieve you," continued Fred, removing the clotted hair, etcetera, in a few seconds, and applying a cleansing lotion. "I cut it off, you see, just as the Great Physician cuts away our sins, and washes us clean in the fountain of His own blood. You feel better already, don't you?"

"There's no doubt about that," replied the patient looking up with a great sigh of relief that told far more than words could convey.

We will not record all that was said and done upon that occasion. Let it suffice to say that the man's wound was put in a fair way of recovery without the expense and prolonged suffering of a trip home.

Thereafter, as a breeze was beginning to blow which bid fair to become a "fishing breeze," it became necessary for the visitors to leave in haste, but not before a few books, tracts, and worsted mittens had been distributed, with an earnest invitation from the skipper of the *Sunbeam* to every one to repeat the visit whenever calm weather should permit, and especially on Sundays, when regular

R. M. Ballantyne

services would be held on deck or in the hold.

On this occasion Bob Lumpy and Pat Stiver had met and joined hands in great delight, not unmingled with surprise.

"Well, who'd ever have expected to find *you* here?" said Bob.

"Ah, who indeed?" echoed Pat. "The fact is, I came to be near *you*, Bob."

"But how did it happen? Who got you the sitivation? Look alive! Don't be long-winded, I see they're gittin' our boat ready."

"This is 'ow it was, Bob. I was shovin' Eve about the roads in the bath-chair, as you know I've bin doin' ever since I entered your service, w'en a gen'lem'n come up and axed all about us. 'Would ye like a sitivation among the North Sea fishermen?' says he. 'The very ticket,' says I. 'Come to Lun'on to-night, then,' says he. 'Unpossible,' says I, fit to bu'st wi' disappointment; "cos I must first shove Miss Eve home, an' git hold of a noo shover to take my place.' 'All right,' says he, laughin'; 'come when you can. Here's my address.' So away I goes; got a trustworthy, promisin' young feller as I've know'd a long time to engage for Miss Eve, an' off to Lun'on, an'—here I am!"

"Time's up," cried the Admiral at this point, shaking hands with Fred Martin; while Bob Lumsden sprang from the side of his little friend, and there was a general move towards the boats.

"Good-bye, mate," said Skipper Fox, holding out his hand.

"Stop, friends," cried Fred, in a loud voice; "that's not the way we part on board o' the *Sunbeam*."

Taking off his hat and looking up,—a sign that all understood, for they immediately uncovered and bowed their heads,—the missionary skipper, in a few brief but earnest words, asked for a blessing on the work which he had been privileged that day to begin, that Satan might be foiled, and the name of Jesus be made precious among the fishermen of the North Sea.

Thereafter the boats scattered towards their various smacks, their crews rejoicing in this latest addition to the fleet. Even Groggy Fox gave it as his opinion that there might be worse things after all in the world than "mission wessels!"

R. M. Ballantyne

CHAPTER NINE

BEGINNING OF THE GOOD WORK

The breeze which had begun to blow freshened as the day advanced, and the Admiral, directing his course to the nor'-east, made for the neighbourhood of the Dogger Bank. Having reached what he deemed suitable fishing-ground, he changed his course and gave the signal to "put to." With the precision of well-trained troops the smacks obeyed, and let down their trawls. The *Sunbeam* also let down her net, and shaped her course like the rest, thus setting an example of attention to secular duty. She trawled for fish so as to help to pay expenses, until such time as suitable weather and opportunity offered for the main and higher duty of fishing for men.

The first haul of the mission vessel was a great success, prophetic of the great successes in store, thought her skipper, as the cod-end was finally swung inboard in an almost bursting condition. When the lower end was opened, and the living fountain of fish gushed over the deck, there was a general exclamation of satisfaction, mingled with thanksgiving, from the crew, for fishes great and small were there in abundance of every sort that swims in the North Sea.

"All sorts and conditions of men" leaped into Fred Martin's mind, for he was thinking of higher things at the moment. "A good beginning and a good omen," he murmured.

"*Wot* a haul!" exclaimed Pat Stiver, who was nearly swept off his legs, and to whom the whole thing was an entirely new experience.

"Use your eyes less and your hands more, my boy," said Fink, the mate, setting the example by catching hold of a magnificent turbot that would have graced a lord mayor's feast, and commencing to clean it.

Pat was by no means a lazy boy. Recovering from his surprise, he set to work with all the vigour of a man of purpose, and joined the rest of the crew in their somewhat disagreeable duty.

They wrought with such goodwill that their contribution of trunks to the general supply was the largest put on board the steamer next day.

Calm and storm sometimes succeed each other rapidly on the North Sea. It was so on the present occasion. Before the nets could be cleared and let down for another take, the breeze had died away. The weather that was unsuited, however, for fishing, was very suitable for "ferrying" to the steamer; and when that all-important duty was done, the comparative calm that prevailed was just the thing for the work of the *Sunbeam*.

Well aware of this, Manx Bradley and other like-minded skippers, kept close to the mission ship, whose great blue flag was waving welcome to all. Boats were soon pulling towards her, their crews being influenced by a great

R. M. Ballantyne

variety of motives; and many men who, but for her presence, would have been gambling or drinking, or oppressed with having nothing to do, or whistling for a breeze, found an agreeable place of meeting on her deck.

On this occasion a considerable number of men who had received slight injuries from accidents came on board, so that Fred had to devote much of his time to the medical part of his work, while Fink, his mate, superintended the distribution of what may be styled worsted-works and literature.

"Hallo, Jim Freeman!" said Fred, looking round from the medicine shelves before which he stood searching for some drug; "you're the very man I want to see. Want to tempt you away from Skipper Lockley, an' ship with me in the *Sunbeam*."

"I'm not worth much for anybody just now," said Freeman, holding up his right hand, which was bound in a bloody handkerchief. "See, I've got what'll make me useless for weeks to come, I fear."

"Never fear, Jim," said Fred, examining the injured member, which was severely bruised and lacerated. "How got ye that?"

"Carelessness, Fred. The old story—clapped my hand on the gunwale o' the boat when we were alongside the carrier."

"I'd change with 'ee, Jim, if I could," growled Joe Stubley, one of the group of invalids who filled the cabin at the time.

There was a general laugh, as much at Joe's lugubrious

visage as at his melancholy tone.

"Why, what's wrong with *you*, Stubs?" asked Fred.

"DT," remarked the skipper of the *Cormorant*, who could hardly speak because of a bad cold, and who thus curtly referred to the drunkard's complaint of *delirium tremens*.

"Nothin' o' the sort!" growled Joe. "I've not seed a *coper* for a week or two. Brandy's more in your way, Groggy Fox, than in mine. No, it's mulligrumps o' some sort that's the matter wi' me."

"Indeed," said Fred, as he continued to dress the bruised hand. "What does it feel like, Stubs?"

"Feel like?" exclaimed the unhappy man, in a tone that told of anguish, "it feels like red-hot thunder rumblin' about inside o' me. Just as if a great conger eel was wallopin' about an' a-dinin' off my witals."

"Horrible, but not incurable," remarked Fred. "I'll give you some pills, boy, that'll soon put you all to rights. Now, then, who's next?"

While another of the invalids stepped forward and revealed his complaints, which were freely commented on by his more or less sympathetic mates, Fink had opened out a bale of worsted comforters, helmets, and mitts on deck, and, assisted by Pat Stiver, was busily engaged in distributing them. "Here you are—a splendid pair of mitts, Jack," he said, tossing the articles to a huge man, who received them with evident satisfaction.

"Too small, I fear," said Jack, trying to force his enormous hand into one of them.

R. M. Ballantyne

"Hold on! don't bu'st it!" exclaimed Pat sharply; there's all sorts and sizes here. "There's a pair, now, that would fit Goliath."

"Ah, them's more like it, little 'un," cried the big fisherman. "No more sea-blisters now, thanks to the ladies on shore," he added, as he drew the soft mittens over his sadly scarred wrists.

"Now then, who wants this?" continued Fink, holding up a worsted helmet; "splendid for the back o' the head and neck, with a hole in front to let the eyes and nose out."

"Hand over," cried David Duffy.

"I say, wot's this inside?" exclaimed one of the men, drawing a folded paper from one of his mittens and opening it.

"Read, an' you'll maybe find out," suggested the mate.

"'God, who giveth us richly all things to enjoy,'" said the fisherman, reading from the paper.

"Just so," said Fink, "that's what the lady as made the mitts wants to let you know so's you may larn to think more o' the Giver than the gifts."

"I wish," said another of the men testily, as he pulled a tract from inside one of his mitts, and flung it on the deck, "I wish as how these same ladies would let religion alone, an' send us them things without it. We want the mitts, an' comforters, an' helmets, but we don't want their humbuggin' religion."

"Shame, Dick!" said David Duffy, as he wound a

comforter round his thick neck. "You shouldn't look a gift horse in the mouth. We're bound to take the things as they've been sent to us, an' say 'Thank 'ee.'"

"If it wasn't for what you call 'humbuggin' religion,'" remarked Fink, looking Dick straight in the face, "it's little that we'd see o' comforters, or books, or mission ships on the North Sea. Why, d'ee think that selfishness, or greed, or miserliness, or indifference, or godlessness would ever take the trouble to send all them things to us? Can't you understand that the love of God in the heart makes men and women wish to try to keep God's commandments by bein' kind to one another, an' considering the poor, an' feedin' the hungry, an' clothin' the naked?"

"Right you are, Fink," said Lockley, with a nod of approval, which was repeated by several of those around.

"But, I say, you spoke of books, mate," remarked Bob Lumsden, who came forward at the moment, much to the satisfaction of his little friend Pat Stiver; "you han't showed us any books yet."

"One thing at a time, boy," returned the mate.

"We've got lots o' books too. Go below, Pat, an' ask the skipper to send up that big case o' books; say I've about finished givin' out the mitts an' mufflers."

"Just so, boy," put in his friend Bob; "say that the mate has distributed the soft goods, an' wants some hard facts now."

"Don't be cheeky, you young rascal!" cried the mate, hitting Bob on the nose with a well aimed pair of mittens.

R. M. Ballantyne

"Thankee! On'y them things was meant for the hands not for the nose. Howsever, I won't quarrel with a gift, no matter what way it comes to me," retorted Bob, picking up the mitts and putting them in his pocket.

While he was speaking two men brought on deck a large box, which was quickly opened by the mate. The men crowded around with much interest and curiosity, for it was the first batch of books that had ever reached that fleet. The case was stuffed to the lid with old periodicals and volumes, of every shape, and size, and colour.

"W'y, they've bin an' sent us the whole British Museum, I do believe!" exclaimed David Duffy, whose younger brother chanced to be a porter in our great storehouse of literature.

"Here you are, lads!" cried Fink, going down on his knees and pulling out the contents. "Wollum of *The Leisure Hour, Sunday Magazine*, odd numbers o' *The Quiver*, wollum of *The Boy's Own Paper, Young England, Home Words*, and *Good Words* (to smother our bad words, you know). There you are, enough to make doctors or professors of every man Jack o' you, if you'll on'y take it all in."

"Professors!" growled Joe Stubley, who had come on deck, still suffering from his strange internal complaint. "More like to make fools on us. Wot do *we* want wi' books and larnin'!"

"Nothin' wotsumdever," answered Pat Stiver, with a look of the most patronising insolence. "You're right, Joe, quite right—as you always are. Smacksmen has got no souls, no brains, no minds, no hintellects."

"They've got no use for books, bless you! All they wants is wittles an' grog—"

The boy pulled up at this point, for Stubley made a rush at him, but Pat was too quick for him.

"Well said, youngster; give it him hot," cried one of the men approvingly, while the others laughed; but they were too much interested in the books to be diverted from these for more than a few seconds. Many of them were down on their knees beside the mate, who continued in a semi-jocular strain—"Now then, take your time, my hearties; lots o' books here, and lots more where these came from. The British public will never run dry. I'm cheap John! Here they are, all for nothin', *on loan*; small wollum—the title ain't clear, ah!—*The Little Man as Lost his Mother*; big wollum—*Shakespeare; Pickwick*; books by Hesba Stretton; Almanac; Missionary Williams; *Polar Seas an' Regions; Pilgrim's Progress*—all sorts to suit all tastes—Catechisms, Noo Testaments, *Robinson Crusoe*."

"Hold on there, mate; let's have a look at that!" cried Bob Lumsden eagerly—so eagerly that the mate handed the book to him with a laugh.

"Come here, Pat," whispered Bob, dragging his friend out of the crowd to a retired spot beside the boat of the *Sunbeam*, which lay on deck near the mainmast. "Did you ever read *Robinson Crusoe*?"

"No, never—never so much as 'eard of 'im."

"You can read, I suppose?"

"Oh yes; I can read well enough."

"What have you read?" demanded Bob.

"On'y bits of old noospapers," replied Pat, with a look of contempt, "an' I don't like readin'."

"Don't like it? Of course you don't, you ignorant curmudgeon, if noospapers is all you've read. Now, Pat, I got this book, not for myself but a purpus for *you*."

"Thankee for nothin'," said Pat; "I doesn't want it."

"Doesn't want it!" repeated Bob. "D'ee know that this is the very best book as ever was written?"

"You seems pretty cock-sure," returned Pat, who was in a contradictory mood that day; "but you know scholards sometimes differ in their opinions about books."

"Pat I'll be hard upon you just now if you don't look out!" said Bob seriously. "Howsever, you're not so far wrong, arter all. People *does* differ about books, so I'll only say that *Robinson Crusoe* is the best book as was ever written, in *my* opinion, an' so it'll be in yours, too, when you have read it; for there's shipwrecks, an' desert islands, an' savages, an' scrimmages, an' footprints, an'—see here! That's a pictur of him in his hairy dress, wi' his goat, an' parrot, an' the umbrellar as he made hisself, a-lookin' at the footprint on the sand."

The picture, coupled with Bob Lumsden's graphic descryption, had the desired effect. His little friend's interest was aroused, and Pat finally accepted the book, with a promise to read it carefully when he should find time.

"But of that," added Pat, "I ain't got too much on hand."

"You've got all that's of it—four and twenty hours, haven't you?" demanded his friend.

"True, Bob, but it's the *spare* time I'm short of. Howsever, I'll do my best."

While this literary conversation was going on beside the boat, the visitors to the *Sunbeam* had been provided with a good supply of food for the mind as well as ease and comfort for the body, and you may be very sure that the skipper and his men, all of whom were Christians, did not fail in regard to the main part of their mission, namely, to drop in seeds of truth as they found occasion, which might afterwards bear fruit to the glory of God and the good of man.

R. M. Ballantyne

CHAPTER TEN

THE FIRST FIGHT AND VICTORY

There was on board the *Sunbeam*, on this her first voyage, a tall, broad-shouldered, but delicate-looking young man, with a most woebegone expression and a yellowish-green countenance. To look at him was to pronounce him a melancholy misanthrope—a man of no heart or imagination.

Never before, probably, did a man's looks so belie his true character. This youth was an enthusiast; an eager, earnest, hearty Christian, full of love to his Master and to all mankind, and a student for the ministry. But John Binning had broken down from over-study, and at the time we introduce him to the reader he was still further "down" with that most horrible complaint, sea-sickness.

Even when in the depth of his woe at this time, some flashes of Binning's true spirit gleamed fitfully through his misery. One of those gleams was on the occasion of Dick Martin being rescued. Up to that period, since leaving Yarmouth, Binning had lain flat on his back. On hearing of the accident and the rescue he had turned out manfully and tried to speak to the rescued man, but indescribable sensations quickly forced him to retire.

Again, when the first visitors began to sing one of his favourite hymns, he leaped up with a thrill of emotion in his heart, but somehow the thrill went to his stomach, and he collapsed.

At last however, Neptune appeared to take pity on the poor student. His recovery—at least as regarded the sea-sickness—was sudden. He awoke, on the morning after the opening of the case of books, quite restored. He could hardly believe it. His head no longer swam; other parts of him no longer heaved. The first intimation that Skipper Martin had of the change was John Binning bursting into a hymn with the voice of a stentor. He rose and donned his clothes.

"You've got your sea legs at last, sir," said Fred Martin, as Binning came on deck and staggered towards him with a joyful salutation.

"Yes, and I've got my sea appetite, too, Mr Martin. Will breakfast be ready soon?"

"Just goin' on the table, sir. I like to hear that question. It's always a sure and good sign."

At that moment Pat Stiver appeared walking at an acute angle with the deck, and bearing a dish of smoking turbot. He dived, as it were, into the cabin without breaking the dish, and set it on the very small table, on which tea, bread, butter, and a lump of beef were soon placed beside it. To this sumptuous repast the skipper, the student, and the mate sat down. After a very brief prayer for blessing by the skipper, they set to work with a zest which perhaps few but seafaring men can fully understand. The student, in particular, became irrepressible after the first silent and ravenous attack.

R. M. Ballantyne

"Oh!" he exclaimed, "the sea! the sea! the open sea! If you are ill, go to sea. If you are fagged, go to sea! If you are used up, seedy, washed-out, miserable, go to sea! Another slice of that turbot, please. Thanks."

"Mind your cup, sir," said the skipper, a few minutes after, in a warning voice; "with a breeze like this it's apt to pitch into your lap. She lays over a good deal because I've got a press of sail on her this morning."

"More than usual?" asked Binning.

"Yes. You see I'm trying to beat a *coper* that's close ahead of us just now. The *Sunbeam* is pretty swift on her heels, an' if the breeze holds—ha! you've got it, sir?"

He certainly had got it, in his lap—where neither cup, saucer, nor tea should be.

"You are right, skipper, and if your ready hands had not prevented it I should have got the teapot and sugar-basin also. But no matter. As I've had enough now, I'll go on deck and walk myself dry."

On deck a new subject of interest occupied the mind of the rapidly reviving student, for the race between the *Sunbeam* and the *coper* was not yet decided. They were trying which would be first to reach a group of smacks that were sailing at a considerable distance ahead on the port bow. At first the *coper* seemed to have the best of it, but afterwards the breeze freshened and the *Sunbeam* soon left it far astern. Seeing that the race was lost, the floating grog-shop changed her course.

"Ah, she'll steer for other fleets where there's no opposition," remarked the skipper.

"To win our first race is a good omen," said John Binning, with much satisfaction. "May the *copers* be thus beaten from every fleet until they are beaten from the North Sea altogether!"

"Amen to that," said Fred Martin heartily. "You feel well enough now, sir, to think of undertaking service to-morrow, don't you?"

"Think of it, my friend! I have done more than think," exclaimed the student; "I have been busy while in bed preparing for the Sabbath, and if the Master sends us calm weather I will surely help in the good work you have begun so well."

And the Master did send calm weather—so calm and so beautiful that the glassy sea and fresh air and bright blue sky seemed typical of the quiet "rest that remaineth for the people of God." Indeed, the young student was led to choose that very text for his sermon, ignoring all his previous preparation, so impressed was he with the suitability of the theme. And when afterwards the boats of the various smacks came trooping over the sea, and formed a long tail astern of the *Sunbeam*, and when the capacious hold was cleared, and packed as full as possible with rugged weather-beaten men, who looked at the tall pale youth with their earnest inquiring gaze, like hungering men who had come there for something and would not be content to depart with nothing, the student still felt convinced that his text was suitable, although not a single word or idea regarding it had yet struggled in his mind to get free.

In fact the young man's mind was like a pent-up torrent, calm for the moment, but with tremendous and ever-increasing force behind the flood-gates, for he had before

R. M. Ballantyne

him men, many of whom had scarcely ever heard the Gospel in their lives, whose minds were probably free from the peculiar prejudices of landsmen, whose lives were spent in harsh, hard, cheerless toil, and who stood sorely in need of spiritual rest and deliverance from the death of sin. Many of these men had come there only out of curiosity; a few because they loved the Lord, and some because they had nothing better to do.

Groggy Fox was among them. He had come as before for "baccy," forgetting that the weed was not sold on Sundays, and had been prevailed on to remain to the service. Dick Martin was also there, in a retired and dark corner. He was curious to know, he remarked, what the young man had to talk about.

It was not till after prayer had been offered by the student that God opened the flood-gates. Then the stream gushed forth.

"It is," said the preacher—in tones not loud, but so deep and impressive that every soul was at once enthralled—"it is to the servants of the devil that the grand message comes. Not to the good, and pure, and holy is the blessed Gospel or good news sent, but, to the guilty, the sin-stricken, the bad, and the sin-weary God has sent by His blessed Spirit the good and glorious news that there is deliverance in Jesus Christ for the chief of sinners. Deliverance from sin changes godless men into the children of God, and there is *rest* for these. Do I need to tell toilers of the deep how sweet rest is to the tired-out body? Surely not, because you have felt it, and know all about it better than I do. But it *is* needful to tell you about rest for the soul, because some of you have never felt it, and know not what it is. Is there no man before me who has, some time or other, committed some grievous sin, whose soul groans under the burden of the thought, and who would give all he possesses if he had never put out his hand to commit that sin? Is there no one here under the power of that deadly monster—strong drink—who, remembering the days when he was free from bondage, would sing this day with joy unspeakable if he could only escape?"

"Yes," shouted a strong voice from a dark corner of the hold. "Thank God!" murmured another voice from a different quarter, for there were men in that vessel's hold who were longing for the salvation of other as well as their own souls.

No notice was taken of the interrupters. The preacher only paused for an instant as if to emphasise the words—"Jesus Christ is able to save to the *uttermost* all who come to God through Him."

We will not dwell on this subject further than to say that the prayer which followed the sermon was fervent and short, for that student evidently did not think that he should be "heard for his much speaking!" The prayer which was thereafter offered by the Admiral of the fleet was still shorter, very much to the point, and replete with nautical phrases, but an uncalled-for petition, which followed that, was briefest of all. It came in low but distinct tones from a dark corner of the hold, and had a powerful effect on the audience; perhaps, also, on the Hearer of prayer. It was merely—"God have mercy on me."

Whatever influence might have resulted from the preaching and the prayer on that occasion, there could be no doubt whatever as to the singing. It was tremendous! The well-known powers of Wesleyan throats would have been lost in it. Saint Paul's Cathedral organ could not have drowned it. Many of the men had learned at least the tunes of the more popular of Sankey's hymns, first from the Admiral and a few like-minded men, then from each other. Now every man was furnished with an orange-coloured booklet. Some could read; some could not. It mattered little. Their hearts had been stirred by that young student, or rather by the student's God. Their voices, trained to battle with the tempest, formed a safety-valve to their feelings. "The Lifeboat" was, appropriately, the first hymn chosen. Manx Bradley led with a voice like a trumpet, for joy intensified his powers. Fred Martin broke forth with tremendous energy. It was catching. Even Groggy Fox was overcome. With eyes shut, mouth wide open, and book upside down, he absolutely howled his determination to "leave the poor old stranded wreck, and pull for the shore."

But skipper Fox was not the only man whose spirit was touched on that occasion. Many of the boats clung to the mission vessel till the day was nearly past, for their crews were loath to part. New joys, new hopes, new sensations had been aroused. Before leaving, Dick Martin took John Binning aside, and in a low but firm voice said—"you're right, sir. A grievous sin *does* lie heavy on me. I robbed Mrs Mooney, a poor widdy, of her little bag o' savin's—twenty pounds it was."

The latter part of this confession was accidentally overheard by Bob Lumsden. He longed to hear more, but Bob had been taught somehow that eavesdropping is a mean and dishonourable thing. With manly determination, therefore, he left the spot, but immediately sought and found his little friend Pat Stiver, intent on relieving his feelings.

"What d'ee think, Pat?" he exclaimed, in a low whisper, but with indignation in his eye and tone.

"I ain't thinkin' at all," said Pat.

"Would you believe it, Pat?" continued Bob, "I've just heerd that scoun'rel Dick Martin say that it *was* him as stole the money from Mrs Mooney—from the mother of our Eve!"

"You *don't* say so!" exclaimed Pat, making his eyes remarkably wide and round.

"Yes, I does, an' I've long suspected him. Whether he was boastin' or not I can't tell, an' it do seem strange that he should boast of it to the young parson—leastwise, unless it was done to spite him. But now mark me, Pat Stiver, I'll bring that old sinner to his marrow-bones before long, and make him disgorge too, if he hain't spent it all. I give you leave to make an Irish stew o' my carcase if I don't. Ay, ay, sir!"

The concluding words of Bob Lumsden's speech were in reply to an order from Skipper Lockley to haul the boat alongside. In a few minutes more the mission ship was forsaken by her strange Sabbath congregation, and left with all the fleet around her floating quietly on the tranquil sea.

R. M. Ballantyne

CHAPTER ELEVEN

A CONSULTATION, A FEAST, AND A PLOT

There was—probably still is—a coffee-tavern in Gorleston where, in a cleanly, cheerful room, a retired fisherman and his wife, of temperance principles, supplied people with those hot liquids which are said to cheer without inebriating.

Here, by appointment, two friends met to discuss matters of grave importance. One was Bob Lumsden, the other his friend and admirer Pat Stiver. Having asked for and obtained two large cups of coffee and two slices of buttered bread for some ridiculously small sum of money, they retired to the most distant corner of the room, and, turning their backs on the counter, began their discussion in low tones.

Being early in the day, the room had no occupants but themselves and the fisherman's wife, who busied herself in cleaning and arranging plates, cups, and saucers, etcetera, for expected visitors.

"Pat," said Bob, sipping his coffee with an appreciative air, "I've turned a total abstainer."

"W'ich means?" inquired Pat.

"That I don't drink nothin' at all," replied Bob.

"But you're a-drinkin' now!" said Pat.

"You know what I mean, you small willain; I drink nothin' with spirits in it."

"Well, I don't see what you gains by that, Bob, for I heerd Fred Martin say you was nat'rally 'full o' spirit,' so abstainin' 'll make no difference."

"Pat," said Bob sternly, "if you don't clap a stopper on your tongue, I'll wollop you."

Pat became grave at once. "Well, d'ee know, Bob," he said, with an earnest look, "I do b'lieve you are right. You've always seemed to me as if you had a sort o' dissipated look, an' would go to the bad right off if you gave way to drink. Yes, you're right, an' to prove my regard for you I'll become a total abstainer too—but, nevertheless, I *can't* leave off drinkin'."

"Can't leave off drinkin'!" echoed Bob.

Pat shook his head. "No—can't. 'Taint possible."

"Why, wot *do* you mean?"

"Well, Bob, I mean that as I've never yet begun to drink, it ain't possible for me to leave it off, d'ee see, though I was to try ever so hard. Howsever, I'll become an abstainer all the same, just to keep company along wi' you."

Bob Lumsden gave a short laugh, and then, resuming his

earnest air, said—

"Pat, I've found out that Dick Martin, the scoun'rel, has bin to Mrs Mooney's hut again, an' now I'm sartin sure it was him as stole the 'ooman's money—not because I heerd him say so to Mr Binning, but because Eve told me she saw him flattenin' his ugly nose against her window-pane last night, an' recognised him at once for the thief. Moreover, he opened the door an' looked into the room, but seein' that he had given Eve a terrible fright, he drew back smartly an' went away."

"The willain!" exclaimed Pat Stiver, snapping his teeth as if he wanted to bite, and doubling up his little fists. It was evident that Bob's news had taken away all his tendency to jest.

"Now it's plain to me," continued Bob, "that the willain means more mischief. P'r'aps he thinks the old 'ooman's got more blunt hid away in her chest, or in the cupboard. Anyhow, he's likely to frighten poor Eve out of her wits, so it's my business to stop his little game. The question is, how is it to be done. D'ee think it would be of any use to commoonicate wi' the police?"

The shaking of Pat Stiver's head was a most emphatic answer.

"No," said he, "wotiver you do, have nothin' to do wi' the p'leece. They're a low-minded, pig-headed set, wi' their 'move on's,' an' their 'now then, little un's;' an' their grabbin's of your collars, without no regard to w'ether they're clean or not, an' their—"

"Let alone the police, Pat," interrupted his friend, "but let's have your adwice about what should be done."

After a moment's consideration, the small boy advised that Mrs Mooney's hut should be watched.

"In course," he said, "Dick Martin ain't such a fool as to go an' steal doorin' the daytime, so we don't need to begin till near dark. You are big an' strong enough now, Bob, to go at a man like Dick an' floor him wi a thumpin' stick."

"Scarcely," returned Bob, with a gratified yet dubious shake of his head. "I'm game to try, but it won't do to risk gettin' the worst of it in a thing o' this sort."

"Well, but if I'm there with another thumpin' stick to back you up," said Pat, "you'll have no difficulty wotsumdever. An' then, if we should need help, ain't the 'Blue Boar' handy, an' there's always a lot o' hands there ready for a spree at short notice? Now, my adwice is that we go right off an' buy two thumpin' sticks—yaller ones, wi' big heads like Jack the Giant Killer—get 'em for sixpence apiece. A heavy expense, no doubt, but worth goin' in for, for the sake of Eve Mooney. And when, in the words o' the old song, the shades of evenin' is closin' o'er us, we'll surround the house of Eve, and 'wait till the brute rolls by!'"

"You're far too poetical, Pat, for a practical man, said his friend. "Howsomediver, I think, on the whole, your adwice is not bad, so well try it on. But wot are we to do till the shades of evenin' comes on?"

"Amoose ourselves," answered Pat promptly.

"H'm! might do worse," returned his friend. "I s'pose you know I've got to be at Widow Martin's to take tea wi' Fred an' his bride on their return from their weddin' trip. I wonder if I might take you with me, Pat. You're small, an'

R. M. Ballantyne

I suppose you don't eat much."

"Oh, don't I, though?" exclaimed Pat.

"Well, no matter. It would be very jolly. We'd have a good blow-out, you know; sit there comfortably together till it began to git dark, and then start off to—to—"

"Go in an' win," suggested the little one.

Having thus discussed their plans and finished their coffee, the two chivalrous lads went off to Yarmouth and purchased two of the most formidable cudgels they could find, of the true Jack-the-Giant-Killer type, with which they retired to the Denes to "amoose" themselves.

Evening found them hungry and hearty at the tea-table of Mrs Martin—and really, for the table of a fisherman's widow, it was spread with a very sumptuous repast; for it was a great day in the history of the Martin family. No fewer than three Mrs Martins were seated round it. There was old Granny Martin, who consented to quit her attic window on that occasion and take the head of the table, though she did so with a little sigh, and a soft remark that, "It would be sad if he were to come when she was not watching." Then there was widow Martin, Fred's mother—whose bad leg, by the way, had been quite cured by her legacy.

And lastly, there was pretty Mrs Isa Martin, Fred's newly-married wife.

Besides these there were skipper Lockley of the *Lively Poll*, and his wife Martha—for it will be remembered Martha was cousin to Isa, and Stephen's smack chanced to be in port at this time as well as the *Sunbeam* and the

Fairy, alias the *Ironclad*, which last circumstance accounts for Dick Martin being also on shore. But Dick was not invited to this family gathering, for the good reason that he had not shown face since landing, and no one seemed to grieve over his absence, with the exception of poor old granny, whose love for her "wandering boy" was as strong and unwavering as was her love to the husband, for whose coming she had watched so long.

Bob Lumsden, it may be remarked, was one of the guests, because Lockley was fond of him; and Pat Stiver was there because Bob was fond of *him*! Both were heartily welcomed.

Besides the improvement in Mrs Martin's health, there was also vast improvement in the furniture and general appearance of the attic since the arrival of the legacy.

"It was quite a windfall," remarked Mrs Lockley, handing in her cup for more tea.

"True, Martha, though I prefer to call it a godsend," said Mrs Martin. "You see it was gettin' so bad, what wi' standin' so long at the tub, an' goin' about wi' the clo'es, that I felt as if I should break down altogether, I really did; but now I've been able to rest it I feel as if it was going to get quite strong again, and that makes me fit to look after mother far better. Have some more tea, granny!"

A mumbled assent and a pleased look showed that the old woman was fully alive to what was going on.

"Hand the butter to Isa, Pat. Thankee," said the ex-washerwoman. "What a nice little boy your friend is, Bob Lumpy! I'm so glad you thought of bringin' him. He quite puts me in mind of what my boy Fred was at his age—on'y a trifle broader, an' taller, an stouter."

"A sort of lock-stock-an'-barrel difference, mother," said Fred, laughing.

"I dun know what you mean by your blocks, stocks, an' barrels," returned Mrs Martin, "but Pat is a sight milder in the face than you was, an I'm sure he's a better boy."

The subject of this remark cocked his ears and winked gently with one eye to his friend Bob, with such a sly look that the blooming bride, who observed it, went off into a shriek of laughter.

"An' only to think," continued Mrs Martin, gazing in undisguised admiration at her daughter-in-law, "that my Fred—who seems as if on'y yesterday he was no bigger than Pat, should have got Isa Wentworth—the best lass in all Gorleston—for a wife! You're a lucky boy!"

"Right you are," responded Fred, with enthusiasm. "I go wi' you there, mother, but I'm more than a lucky boy—I'm a highly favoured one, and I thank God for the precious gift; and also for that other gift, which is second only to Isa, the command of a Gospel ship on the North Sea."

A decided chuckle, which sounded like a choke, from granny, fortunately called for attentions from the bride at this point.

"But do 'ee really think your mission smack will do much good?" asked Martha Lockley, who was inclined to scepticism.

"I am sure of it," replied Fred emphatically. "Why, we've

done some good work already, though we have bin but a short time wi' the fleet. I won't speak of ourselves, but just look at what has bin done in the way of saving drunkards and swearers by the *Cholmondeley* in the short-Blue Fleet, and by the old *Ensign* in the Fleet started by Mr Burdett-Coutts, the *Columbia* fleet, and in the other fleets that have got Gospel ships. It is not too much to say that there are hundreds of men now prayin' to God, singin' the praises o' the Lamb, an' servin' their owners better than they ever did before, who not long ago were godless drunkards and swearers."

"Men are sometimes hypocrites," objected Martha; "how d'ee know that they are honest, or that it will last?"

"Hypocrites?" exclaimed Fred, pulling a paper hastily from his pocket and unfolding it. "I think you'll admit that sharp men o' bussiness are pretty good judges o' hypocrites as well as of good men. Listen to what one of the largest firms of smack-owners says: 'Our men have been completely revolutionised, and we gladly become subscribers of ten guineas to the funds of the Mission.' Another firm says, 'What we have stated does not convey anything like our sense of the importance of the work you have undertaken.'"

"Ay, there's something in that," said Martha, who, like all sceptics, was slow to admit truth.

We say not this to the discredit of sceptics. On the contrary, we think that people who swallow what is called "truth" too easily, are apt to imbibe a deal of error along with it. Doubtless it was for the benefit of such that the word was given—"Prove all things. Hold fast that which is good."

Fred then went to show the immense blessing that mission ships had already been to the North Sea fishermen—alike to their souls and bodies; but we may not follow him further, for Bob Lumsden and Pat Stiver claim individual attention just now.

When these enterprising heroes observed that the shades of evening were beginning to fall, they rose to take their leave.

"Why so soon away, lads?" asked Fred.

"We're goin' to see Eve Mooney," answered Bob. "Whatever are the boys goin' to do wi' them thick sticks?" exclaimed Martha Lockley.

"Fit main an fore masts into a man-o'-war, I suppose," suggested her husband.

The boys did not explain, but went off laughing, and Lockley called after them—

"Tell Eve I've got a rare lot o' queer things for her this trip."

"And give her my dear love," cried Mrs Fred Martin.

"Ay, ay," replied the boys as they hurried away on their self-imposed mission.

CHAPTER TWELVE

THE ENTERPRISE FAILS—REMARKABLY

The lads had to pass the "Blue Boar" on their way to Widow Mooney's hut, and they went in just to see, as Bob said, how the land lay, and whether there was a prospect of help in that quarter if they should require it.

Besides a number of strangers, they found in that den of iniquity Joe Stubley, Ned Bryce, and Groggy Fox—which last had, alas! forgotten his late determination to "leave the poor old stranded wreck and pull for the shore." He and his comrades were still out among the breakers, clinging fondly to the old wreck.

The boys saw at a glance that no assistance was to be expected from these men. Stubley was violently argumentative, Fox was maudlinly sentimental, and Bryce was in an exalted state of heroic resolve. Each sought to gain the attention and sympathy of the other, and all completely failed, but they succeeded in making a tremendous noise, which seemed partially to satisfy them as they drank deeper.

"Come, nothin' to be got here," whispered Bob Lumsden, in a tone of disgust, as he caught hold of his friend's arm.

R. M. Ballantyne

"We'll trust to ourselves—"

"An' the thumpin' sticks," whispered Pat, as they reached the end of the road.

Alas for the success of their enterprise if it had depended on those formidable weapons of war!

When the hut was reached the night had become so nearly dark that they ventured to approach it with the intention of peeping in at the front window, but their steps were suddenly arrested by the sight of a man's figure approaching from the opposite direction. They drew back, and, being in the shadow of a wall, escaped observation. The man advanced noiselessly, and with evident caution, until he reached the window, and peeped in.

"It's Dick," whispered Bob. "Can't see his figure-head, but I know the cut of his jib, even in the dark."

"Let's go at 'im, slick!" whispered Pat, grasping his cudgel and looking fierce.

"Not yet. We must make quite sure, an' nab him in the very act."

As he spoke the man went with stealthy tread to the door of the hut, which the drunken owner had left on the latch. Opening it softly, he went in, shut it after him, and, to the dismay of the boys, locked it on the inside.

"Now, Pat," said Bob, somewhat bitterly, "there's nothin' for it but the police."

Pat expressed strong dissent. "The p'leece," he said, "was useless for real work; they was on'y fit to badger boys an' old women."

"But what can we do?" demanded Bob anxiously, for he felt that time was precious. "You an' I ain't fit to bu'st in the door; an' if we was, Dick would be ready for us. If we're to floor him he must be took by surprise."

"Let's go an' peep," suggested the smaller warrior.

"Come on, then," growled the big one.

The sight that met their eyes when they peeped was indeed one fitted to expand these orbs of vision to the uttermost, for they beheld the thief on his knees beside the invalid's bed, holding her thin hand in his, while his head was bowed upon the ragged counterpane.

Bob Lumsden was speechless.

"Hold me; I'm a-goin' to bu'st," whispered Pat, by way of expressing the depth of his astonishment.

Presently Eve spoke. They could hear her faintly, yet distinctly, through the cracked and patched windows, and listened with all their ears.

"Don't take on so, poor man," she said in her soft loving tones. "Oh, I am *so* glad to hear what you say!"

Dick Martin looked up quickly.

"What!" he exclaimed, "glad to hear me say that I am the thief as stole your mother's money! that I'm a low, vile, selfish blackguard who deserves to be kicked out o' the North Sea fleet—off the face o' the 'arth altogether?"

"Yes," returned Eve, smiling through her tears—for she had been crying—"glad to hear you say all that, because Jesus came to save people like you; but He does not call them such bad names. He only calls them the 'lost.'"

"Well, I suppose you're right, dear child," said the man, after a pause; "an' I do think the Blessed Lord has saved me, for I never before felt as I do now—hatred of my old bad ways, and an *awful* desire to do right for His sake. If any o' my mates had told me I'd feel an' act like this a week ago, I'd have called him a fool. I can't understand it. I suppose that God must have changed me altogether. My only fear is that I'll fall back again into the old bad ways—I'm so helpless for anything good, d'ee see."

"You forget," returned Eve, with another of her tearful smiles; "He says, 'I will never leave thee nor forsake thee'—"

"No, I don't forget that," interrupted Dick quickly; "that is what the young preacher in the mission smack said, an' it has stuck to me. It's that as keeps me up. But I didn't come here to speak about my thoughts an' feelin's," he continued, rising and taking a chair close to the bed, on which he placed a heavy bag. "I come here, Eve, to make restitootion. There's every farthin' I stole from your poor mother. I kep' it intendin' to go to Lun'on, and have a good long spree—so it's all there. You'll give it to her, but don't tell her who stole it. That's a matter 'tween you an' me an' the Almighty. Just you say that the miserable sinner who took it has bin saved by Jesus Christ, an' now returns it and axes her pardon."

Eve gladly promised, but while she was yet speaking, heavy footsteps were heard approaching the hut. The man started up as if to leave, and the two boys, suddenly awakening to the fact that they were eavesdropping, fled silently round the corner of the hut and hid themselves. The passer-by, whoever he was, seemed to change his mind, for the steps ceased to sound for a few moments, then they were heard again, with diminishing force, until they finally died away.

A moment later, and the key was heard to turn, and the door of the hut to open and close, after which the heavy tread of the repentant fisherman was heard as he walked quickly away.

The boys listened in silence till all was perfectly still.

"Well, now," said Bob, drawing a long breath, "who'd have thought that things would have turned out like this?"

"Never heard of sich a case in *my* life before," responded Pat Stiver with emphasis, as if he were a venerable magistrate who had been trying "cases" for the greater part of a long life. "Why, it leaves us nothin' wotiver to do! Even a p'leeceman might manage it! The thief has gone an' took up hisself, tried an' condemned hisself without a jury, pronounced sentance on hisself without a judge, an' all but hanged hisself without Jack Ketch, so there's nothin' for you an' me to do but go an' bury our thumpin' sticks, as Red Injins bury the war-hatchet, retire to our wigwams, an' smoke the pipe of peace."

"Wery good; let's go an' do it, then," returned Bob, curtly.

As it is not a matter of particular interest how the boys reduced this figurative intention to practice, we will leave them, and follow Dick Martin for a few minutes.

His way led him past the "Blue Boar," which at that

moment, however, proved to be no temptation to him. He paused to listen. Sounds of revelry issued from its door, and the voice of Joe Stubley was heard singing with tremendous energy—"Britons, never, never, never, shall be slaves," although he and all his companions were at that very moment thoroughly—in one or two cases almost hopelessly—enslaved to the most terrible tyrant that has ever crushed the human race!

Dick went on, and did not pause till he reached his sister's house. By that time the family party had broken up, but a solitary candle in the attic window showed that old Granny Martin was still on her watch-tower.

"Is that you, Dick?" said his sister, opening to his tap, and letting him in; but there was nothing of welcome or pleasure in the widow's tone.

The fisherman did not expect a warm welcome. He knew that he did not deserve it, but he cared not, for the visit was to his mother. Gliding to her side, he went down on his knees, and laid his rugged head on her lap. Granny did not seem taken by surprise. She laid her withered hand on the head, and said: "Bless you, my boy! I knew you would come, sooner or later; praise be to His blessed name."

We will not detail what passed between the mother and son on that occasion, but the concluding sentence of the old woman was significant: "He can't be long of coming *now*, Dick, for the promises are all fulfilled at last, and I'm ready."

She turned her head slowly again in the old direction, where, across the river and the sands, she could watch the moonbeams glittering on the solemn sea.

Three days later, and the skipper of the *Sunbeam* received a telegram telling him to prepare for guests, two of whom were to accompany him on his trip to the fleet.

It was a bright, warm day when the guests arrived—a dozen or more ladies and gentlemen who sympathised with the Mission, accompanied by the Director.

"All ready for sea, Martin, I suppose?" said the latter, as the party stepped on board from the wharf, alongside of which the vessel lay.

"All ready, sir," responded Fred. "If the wind holds we may be with the fleet, God willing, some time to-morrow night."

The *Sunbeam* was indeed all ready, for the duties on board of her had been performed by those who did their work "as to the Lord, and not to men." Every rope was in its place and properly coiled away, every piece of brass-work about the vessel shone like burnished gold. The deck had been scrubbed to a state of perfect cleanliness, so that, as Jim Freeman said, "you might eat your victuals off it." In short, everything was trim and taut, and the great blue MDSF flag floated from the masthead, intimating that the Gospel ship was about to set forth on her mission of mercy, to fish for men.

Among the party who were conducted by Fred and the Director over the vessel were two clergymen, men of middle age, who had been labouring among all classes on the land: sympathising with the sad, rejoicing with the glad, praying, working, and energising for rich and poor, until health had begun to give way, and change of air and scene had become absolutely necessary. A week or so at the sea, it was thought, would revive them.

R. M. Ballantyne

And what change of air could be more thorough than that from the smoke of the city to the billows of the North Sea? The Director had suggested the change. Men of God were sorely wanted out there, he said, and, while they renewed their health among the fresh breezes of ocean, they might do grand service for the Master among the long-neglected fishermen.

The reasoning seemed just. The offer was kind. The opportunity was good, as well as unique and interesting. The land-worn clergymen accepted the invitation, and were now on their way to the scene of their health-giving work, armed with waterproofs, sou'westers, and sea-boots.

"It will do you good, sir, both body and soul," said Skipper Martin to the elder of the two, when presented to him. "You'll find us a strange lot, sir, out there, but glad to see you, and game to listen to what you've got to say as long as ever you please."

When the visitors had seen all that was to be seen, enjoyed a cup of coffee, prayed and sung with the crew, and wished them God-speed, they went on shore, and the *Sunbeam*, hoisting her sails and shaking out the blue flag, dropped quietly down the river.

Other smacks there were, very much like herself, coming and going, or moored to the wharves, but as the visitors stood on the river bank and waved their adieux, the thought was forced upon them how inconceivably vast was the difference between those vessels which laboured for time and this one which toiled for eternity.

Soon the *Sunbeam* swept out upon the sea, bent over to the freshening breeze, and steered on her beneficent course towards her double fishing-ground.

CHAPTER THIRTEEN

THE TIDE BEGINS TO TURN, AND DEATH STEPS IN

Let us now, good reader, outstrip the *Sunbeam*, and, proceeding to the fleet in advance of her, pay a night visit to one or two of the smacks. We are imaginative creatures, you see, and the powers of imagination are, as you know, almost illimitable. Even now, in fact, we have you hovering over the dark sea, which, however, like the air above it, is absolutely calm, so that the numerous lanterns of the fishing-vessels around are flickering far down into the deep, like gleams of perpendicular lightning.

It is Saturday night, and the particular vessel over which we hover is the *Lively Poll*. Let us descend into her cabin.

A wonderful change has come over the vessel's crew since the advent of the mission smack. Before that vessel joined the fleet, the chief occupation of the men during the hours of leisure was gambling, diversified now and then with stories and songs more or less profane.

On the night of which we write almost universal silence pervaded the smack, because the men were profoundly engaged with book and pamphlet. They could all read,

R. M. Ballantyne

more or less, though the reading of one or two involved much spelling and knitting of the brows. But it was evident that they were deeply interested, and utterly oblivious of all around them. Like a schoolboy with a good story, they could not bear to be interrupted, and were prone to explosive commentary.

David Duffy, who had fallen upon a volume of Dickens, was growing purple in the face, because of his habit of restraining laughter until it forced its way in little squeaks through his nose. Stephen Lockley, who had evidently got hold of something more serious, sat on a locker, his elbows resting on his knees, the book in his hands, and a solemn frown on his face. Hawkson was making desperate efforts to commit to memory a hymn, with the tune of which he had recently fallen in love, and the meaning of which was, unknown to himself, slowly but surely entering deep into his awakening soul. Bob Lumsden, who read his pamphlet by the binnacle light on deck, had secured an American magazine, the humorous style of which, being quite new to him, set him off ever and anon into hearty ripples of laughter.

But they were not equally persevering, for Joe Stubley, to whom reading was more of a toil than a pleasure, soon gave in, and recurred to his favourite game of "checkers." The mate, Peter Jay, was slowly pacing the deck in profound meditation. His soul had been deeply stirred by some of the words which had fallen from the lips of John Binning, and perplexities as well as anxieties were at that time struggling fiercely in his mind.

"Well done, little marchioness!" exclaimed David Duffy, with eyes riveted on his book, and smiting his knee with his right palm, "you're a trump!"

"Shush!" exclaimed Lockley, with eyes also glued to his book, holding up his hand as if to check interruption. "There's somethin' in this, although I can't quite see it yet."

A roar of laughter on deck announced that Bob Lumsden had found something quite to his taste. "First-rate—ha! ha! I wonder if it's all true."

"Hold your noise there," cried Hawkson; "who d'ee think can learn off a hymn wi' you shoutin' like a bo'sun's mate an' Duffy snortin' like a grampus?"

"Ah, just so," chimed in Stubley, looking up from his board. "Why don't you let it out, David? You'll bu'st the b'iler if you don't open a bigger safety-valve than your nose."

"Smack on the weather beam, that looks like the Gospel ship, sir," said the mate, looking down the hatchway.

The skipper closed his book at once and went on deck, but the night was so dark, and the smack in question so far off, that they were unable to make her out among the numerous lights of the fleet.

In another part of that fleet, not far distant, floated the *Cormorant*. Here too, as in many other smacks, the effects of the *Sunbeam's* beneficent influence had begun to tell. Groggy Fox's crew was noted as one of the most quarrelsome and dissipated in the fleet. On this particular Saturday night, however, all was quiet, for most of the men were busy with books, pamphlets, and tracts. One who had, as his mate said, come by a broken head, was slumbering in his berth, scientifically bandaged and convalescent, and Groggy himself, with a pair of

R. M. Ballantyne

tortoiseshell glasses on his nose, was deep in a book which he pronounced to be "one o' the wery best wollums he had ever come across in the whole course of his life," leaving it to be inferred, perhaps, that he had come across a very large number of volumes in his day.

While he was thus engaged one of the men whispered in his ear, "A *coper* alongside, sir."

The skipper shut the "wery best wollum" at once, and ordered out the boat.

"Put a cask o' oysters in her," he said.

Usually his men were eager to go with their skipper, but on this night some of them were so interested in the books they were reading that they preferred to remain on board. Others went, and, with their skipper, got themselves "fuddled" on the proceeds of the owner's oysters. If oysters had not been handy, fish or something else would have been used instead, for Skipper Fox was not particular—he was still clinging to "the poor old stranded wreck."

It was dawn when, according to their appropriate phrase, they "tumbled" over the side of the *coper* into their boat. As they bade the Dutchman good night they observed that he was looking "black as thunder" at the horizon.

"W-wat's wrong, ol' b-boy?" asked Groggy.

The Dutchman pointed to the horizon. "No use for me to shtop here, mit *dat* alongside!" he replied.

The fishermen turned their drunken eyes in the direction indicated, and, after blinking a few seconds, clearly made out the large blue flag, with its letters MDSF, fluttering in the light breeze that had risen with the sun.

With curses both loud and deep the Dutchman trimmed his sails, and slowly but decidedly vanished from the scene. Thus the tide began to turn on the North Sea!

The light breeze went down as the day advanced, and soon the mission vessel found herself surrounded by smacks, with an ever-increasing tail of boats at her stern, and an ever-multiplying congregation on her deck. It was a busy and a lively scene, for while they were assembling, Fred Martin took advantage of the opportunity to distribute books and medicines, and to bind up wounds, etcetera. At the same time the pleasant meeting of friends, who never met in such numbers anywhere else—not even in the *copers*—and the hearty good wishes and shaking of hands, with now and then expressions of thankfulness from believers—all tended to increase the bustle and excitement, so that the two invalid clergymen began at once to experience the recuperative influence of glad enthusiasm.

"There is plenty to do here, both for body and soul," remarked one of these to Fred during a moment of relaxation.

"Yes, sir, thank God. We come out here to work, and we find the work cut out for us. A good many surgical cases, too, you observe. But we expect that. In five of the fleets there were more than two thousand cases treated last year aboard of the mission smacks, so we look for our share. In fact, during our first eight weeks with this fleet we have already had two hundred men applying for medicine or dressing of wounds."

R. M. Ballantyne

"Quite an extensive practice, Dr Martin," said the clergyman, with a laugh.

"Ay, sir; but ours is the medical-missionary line. The body may be first in time, but the soul is first in importance with us."

In proof of this, as it were, the skipper now stopped all that had been going on, and announced that the *real* work of the day was going to begin; whereupon the congergation crowded into the hold until it was full. Those who could not find room clustered on deck round the open hatch and listened—sometimes craned their necks over and gazed.

It was a new experience for the invalid clergymen, who received another bath of recuperative influence. Fervour, interest, intelligence seemed to gleam in the steady eyes of the men while they listened, and thrilled in their resonant voices when they sang. One of the clergymen preached as he had seldom preached before, and then prayed, after which they all sang; but the congregation did not move to go away. The brother clergyman therefore preached, and, modestly fearing that he was keeping them too long, hinted as much.

"Go on, sir," said the Admiral, who was there; "it ain't every day we gets a chance like this."

A murmur of assent followed, and the preacher went on; but we will not follow him. After closing with the hymn, "How sweet the name of Jesus sounds in a believer's ear," they all went on deck, where they found a glory of sunshine flooding the *Sunbeam*, and glittering on the still tranquil sea.

The meeting now resolved itself into a number of groups, among whom the peculiar work of the day was continued directly or indirectly. It was indeed a wonderful condition of things on board of the Gospel ship that Sunday—wheels within wheels, spiritual machinery at work from stem to stern. A few, whose hearts had been lifted up, got out an accordion and their books, and "went in for" hymns. Among these Bob Lumsden and his friend Pat Stiver took an active part. Here and there couples of men leaned over the side and talked to each other in undertones of their Saviour and the life to come. In the bow Manx Bradley got hold of Joe Stubley and pleaded hard with him to come to Jesus, and receive power from the Holy Spirit to enable him to give up all his evil ways. In the stern Fred Martin sought to clear away the doubts and difficulties of Ned Bryce. Elsewhere the two clergymen were answering questions, and guiding several earnest souls to a knowledge of the truth, while down in the cabin Jim Freeman prevailed on several men and boys to sign the temperance pledge. Among these last was Groggy Fox, who, irresolute of purpose, was still holding back.

"'Cause why," said he; "I'll be sure to break it again. I can't keep it."

"I know that, skipper," said Fred, coming down at the moment. "In your own strength you'll *never* keep it, but in God's strength you shall conquer *all* your enemies. Let's pray, lads, that we may all be enabled to keep to our good resolutions."

Then and there they all knelt down, and Skipper Fox arose with the determination once again to "Leave the poor old stranded wreck, and pull for the shore."

R. M. Ballantyne

But that was a memorable Sunday in other respects, for towards the afternoon a stiff breeze sprang up, and an unusually low fall in the barometer turned the fishermen's thoughts back again to wordly cares. The various boats left the *Sunbeam* hurriedly. As the *Lively Poll* had kept close alongside all the time, Stephen Lockley was last to think of leaving. He had been engaged in a deeply interesting conversation with one of the clergymen about his soul, but at last ordered his boat to be hauled alongside.

While this was being done, he observed that another smack—one of the so-called "ironclads"—was sailing so as to cross the bows of his vessel. The breeze had by that time increased considerably, and both smacks, lying well over, were rushing swiftly through the water. Suddenly some part of the ironclad's tackling about the mainsail gave way, the head of the vessel fell to leeward; next moment she went crashing into the *Lively Poll*, and cut her down to the water's edge. The ironclad seemed to rebound and tremble for a moment, and then passed on. The steersman at once threw her up into the wind with the intention of rendering assistance, but in another minute the *Lively Poll* had sunk and disappeared for ever, carrying Peter Jay and Hawkson along with her.

Of course several boats pushed off at once to the rescue, and hovered about the spot for some time, but neither the men nor the vessel were ever seen again.

There was a smack at some distance, which was about to quit the fleet next morning and return to port. The skipper of it knew well which vessel had been run down, but, not being near enough to see all that passed, imagined that the whole crew had perished along with her. During the night the breeze freshened to a gale, which rendered fishing impossible. This vessel therefore left the fleet before dawn, and carried the news to Gorleston that the *Lively Poll* had been run down and sunk with all her crew.

It was Fred Martin's wife who undertook to break this dreadful news to poor Mrs Lockley.

Only those who have had such duty to perform can understand the struggle it cost the gentle-spirited Isa. The first sight of her friend's face suggested to Mrs Lockley the truth, and when words confirmed it she stood for a moment with a countenance pale as death. Then, clasping her hands tightly together, the poor woman, with a cry of despair, sank insensible upon the floor.

CHAPTER FOURTEEN

THE LAST

But the supposed death of Stephen Lockley did not soften the heart of his wife. It only opened her eyes a little. After the first stunning effect had passed, a hard, rebellious state of mind set in, which induced her to dry her tears, and with stern countenance reject the consolation of sympathisers. The poor woman's heart was breaking, and she refused to be comforted.

It was while she was in this condition that Mrs Mooney, of all people, took it into her head to visit and condole with her neighbour. That poor woman, although a sot, was warm-hearted, and the memory of what she had suffered when her own husband perished seemed to arouse her sympathies in an unusual degree. She was, as her male friends would have said, "screwed" when she knocked at Mrs Lockley's door.

The poor creature was recovering from a burst of passionate grief, and turned her large dark eyes fiercely on the would-be comforter as she entered.

"My dear Mrs Lockley," began Mrs Mooney, with sympathy beaming on her red countenance, "it do grieve me to see you like this—a'most as much as wen my—"

"You're drunk!" interrupted Mrs Lockley, with a look of mingled sternness and indignation.

"Well, my dear," replied Mrs Mooney, with a deprecatory smile, "that ain't an uncommon state o' things, an' you've no call to be 'ard on a poor widdy like yourself takin' a little consolation now an' then when she can get it. I just thought I'd like to comfort—"

"I don't want no comfort," cried Mrs Lockley in a sharp tone. "Leave me. Go away!"

There was something so terrible in the mingled look of grief and anger which disturbed the handsome features of the young wife, that Mrs Mooney, partly awed and partly alarmed, turned at once and left the house. She did not feel aggrieved, only astonished and somewhat dismayed. After a few moments of meditation she set off, intending to relieve her feelings in the "Blue Boar." On her way she chanced to meet no less a personage than Pat Stiver, who, with his hands in his pockets and his big boots clattering over the stones, was rolling along in the opposite direction.

"Pat, my boy!" exclaimed the woman in surprise, "wherever did you come from?"

"From the North Sea," said Pat, looking up at his questioner with an inquiring expression. "I say, old woman, drunk again?"

"Well, boy, who denyses of it?"

"Ain't you ashamed of yourself?"

"No, I ain't. Why should I? Who cares whether I'm drunk or sober?"

"Who cares, you unnat'ral old bundle o' dirty clo'es? Don't Eve care? An' don't Fred Martin an' Bob Lumpy care? An' don't *I* care, worse than all of 'em put together, except Eve?"

"You, boy?" exclaimed the woman.

"Yes, me. But look here, old gal; where are you goin'? To have a drink, I suppose?"

"Jus' so. That's 'xactly where I'm a-steerin' to."

"Well, now," cried Pat, seizing the woman's hand, "come along, an' I'll give you somethin' to drink. Moreover, I'll treat you to some noos as'll cause your blood to curdle, an' your flesh to creep, an' your eyes to glare, an your hair to stand on end!"

Thus adjured, and with curiosity somewhat excited, Mrs Mooney suffered herself to be led to that temperance coffee-tavern in Gorleston to which we have already referred.

"Ain't it comfr'able?" asked the boy, as his companion gazed around her. "Now then, missis," he said to the attendant, with the air of an old frequenter of the place, "coffee and wittles for two—hot. Here, sit down in this corner, old lady, where you can take in the beauties o' the place all at one squint."

Almost before he had done speaking two large cups of hot coffee and two thick slices of buttered bread lay before them.

"There you are—all ship-shape. Now drink, an' no heel-taps."

Mrs Mooney drank in dumb surprise, partly at the energy and cool impudence of the boy, and partly at the discovery that there was more comfort in hot coffee than she had expected.

"You've heard, in course, that the *Lively Poll* is at the bottom of the North Sea?" said Pat.

Mrs Mooney set down her cup with a sigh and a sudden expression of woe mingled with reproof, while she remarked that there was no occasion to be lighthearted on such a subject.

"That's all *you* know," retorted Pat. "Of course we was told the moment we came alongside the wharf this mornin', that somebody had bin blowin' half a gale o' lies about it, but Stephen Lockley ain't drownded, not he, an' don't mean to be for some time. He was aboard of the *Sunbeam* at the time his wessel went down an' all the rest of 'em, except poor Jay an' Hawkson, an' we've brought 'em all ashore. You see we got so damaged in a gale that came on to blow the wery next day that we've bin forced to run here for repairs. Skipper Lockley's away up at this here minit to see his wife—leastwise, he's waitin' outside till one o' the parsons goes and breaks the noos to her. The skipper didn't see no occasion for that, an' said he could break the noos to her hisself, but the parson said he didn't know what the consikences might be, so Stephen he gave in, an'—. Now, old girl, if you keep openin' of your mouth an' eyes at that rate you'll git lockjaw, an' never be able to go to sleep no more."

There was, indeed, some ground for the boy's remark, for

his "noos" had evidently overwhelmed Mrs Mooney—chiefly with joy, on account of her friend Mrs Lockley, to whom, even when "in liquor", she was tenderly attached. She continued to gaze speechless at Pat, who took advantage of the opportunity to do a little private business on his own account.

Taking a little bit of blue ribbon with a pin attached to it from his pocket, he coolly fixed it on Mrs Mooney's breast.

"There," said he gravely, "I promised Bob that I'd make as many conwerts as I could, so I've conwerted *you*!"

Utterly regardless of her conversion, Mrs Mooney suddenly sprang from her seat and made for the door.

"Hallo, old gal! where away now!" cried the boy, seizing her skirt and following her out, being unable to stop her.

"I'm a-goin' to tell Eve, an' *won't* she be glad, for she was awful fond o' Lockley!"

"All right, I'm with 'ee. Cut along."

"Mother!" exclaimed Eve, when the poor woman stood before her with eager excitement flushing her face to a ruddy purple. "Have you *really* put on the blue ribbon?"

The poor child's thin pretty little race flushed with hope for a moment.

"Oh, it ain't that, dear," said Mrs Mooney, "but Lockley ain't drownded arter all! He's—he's—"

Here Pat Stiver broke in, and began to explain to the

bewildered girl. He was yet in the midst of his "noos," when the door was flung open, and Mrs Lockley hurried in.

"Forgive me, Mrs Mooney," she cried, grasping her friend's hand, "I shouldn't have spoke to you as I did, but my heart was very sore. Oh, it is breakin'!"

She sat down, covered her face with both hands, and sobbed violently. Her friends stood speechless and helpless. It was obvious that she must have left her house to make this apology before the clergyman who was to break the news had reached it. Before any one could summon courage to speak, a quick step was heard outside, and Lockley himself entered. He had been waiting near at hand for the clergyman to summon him, when he caught sight of his wife entering the hut.

Mrs Lockley sprang up—one glance, a wild shriek, but not of despair— and she would have fallen to the ground had not her husband's strong arms been around her.

It is believed that joy seldom or never kills. At all events it did not kill on this occasion, for Mrs Lockley and her husband were seen that same evening enjoying the hospitality of Mrs Martin, while their little one was being fondled on the knees of the old granny, who pointed through the attic window, and tried to arouse the child's interest in the great sea.

When Mrs Mooney succeeded in turning her attention to the blue ribbon on her breast, she laughed heartily at the idea of such a decoration—much to the sorrow of Eve, who had prayed for many a day, not that her mother might put on that honourable badge, but that she might be brought to the Saviour, in whom are included all things

R. M. Ballantyne

good and true and strong. Nevertheless, it is to be noted that Mrs Mooney did not put the blue ribbon off. She went next day to have a laugh over it with Mrs Lockley. But the fisherman's wife would not laugh. She had found that while sorrow and suffering may drive one to despair in regard to God and self and all terrestrial things, joy frequently softens.

Surely it is the "goodness of God that leadeth to repentance." This life, as it were, from the dead proved to be life from death to herself, and she talked and prayed with her drunken friend until that friend gave her soul to Jesus, and received the Spirit of power by which she was enabled to "hold the fort,"—to adopt and keep the pledge of which her ribbon was but the emblem.

Although we have now described the end of the *Lively Poll*, it must not be supposed that the crew of that ill-fated smack was dispersed and swallowed up among the fishing fleets of the North Sea. On the contrary, though separated for the time, they came together again,—ay, and held together for many a long day thereafter. And this is how it came about.

One morning, a considerable time after the events we have just narrated, Stephen Lockley invited his old comrades to meet him in the Gorleston coffee-tavern, and, over a rousing cup of "hot, with," delivered to them the following oration:

"Friends and former messmates. I ain't much of a speaker, so you'll excuse my goin' to the pint direct. A noble lady with lots o' tin an' a warm heart has presented a smack all complete to our Deep-Sea Fishermen Institootion. It cost, I'm told, about 2000 pounds, and will be ready to start as a Gospel ship next week. For no reason that I knows on, 'xcept that it's the Lord's will, they've appointed me skipper, with directions to choose my own crew. So, lads, I've got you here to ask if you're willin' to ship with me."

"*I'm* willin', of *course*," cried Pat Stiver eagerly, "an so's Bob Lumpy. I'll answer for him!"

There was a general laugh at this, but Bob Lumsden, who was present, chose to answer for himself, and said he was heartily willing. So said David Duffy, and so also said Joe Stubley.

"I on'y wish," added the latter, "that Jim Freeman was free to j'ine, but Fred Martin's not likely to let *him* go, for he's uncommon fond of him."

"He's doin' good work for the Master where he is," returned Lockley, "and we'll manage to catch as true and able a man among the North Sea fleets afore long. There's as good fish in the sea, you know, as ever came out of it. Our mission smack is to be called the *Welcome*."

"At this rate," observed Dick Martin, who was one of the party, "we'll soon have a mission ship to every fleet in the North Sea; that'll please our Director, won't it?"

"Ay, it will," said Lockley. "All the same, I heard the Director say only the other day, he wished people would remember that the mission needed funds to keep the smacks a-goin' as well as to build an' launch 'em. Howsever, we've no need to fear, for when the Master sends the men and the work, He's sure to find the means."

Two weeks after the date on which this harmonious meeting was held, a new vessel, laden with spiritual treasure, unfurled her sails, shook out her MDSF ensign,

R. M. Ballantyne

and, amid the good wishes, silent prayers, and ringing cheers of sympathetic friends on shore, went forth as a beacon of love and light and hope to irradiate the toilers on the dark North Sea.

Among those cheering and praying ones were Mrs Mooney—a brand plucked from the burning—and fragile Eve, with her weak, thin, helpless body and her robust heart, chosen to do herculean and gladiator service of sympathy and rescue in the Master's cause. And you may be sure that blooming Isa Martin was there, and her friend Martha Lockley; Manx Bradley, the Admiral, who, with other fishermen, chanced to be having their spell on shore at that time, was also there. Even old Granny Martin was there, in a sense, for she could see from her attic the great blue flag as it fluttered in the breeze, and she called her unfailing—and no longer ailing daughter to come to the window and look at it and wish it God-speed; after which she turned her old eyes again to their wonted resting-place, where the great sea rolled its crested breakers beyond the sands.

It remains but to add that the *Welcome* was received by the fleet to which she was sent with an enthusiasm which fully justified her name, and that her crew found her thenceforth, both as to her sea-going qualities and the nature of her blessed work, a marvellous improvement on their former home, the *Lively Poll*.

Note. The Office of the Mission to Deep-Sea Fishermen is 181 Queen Victoria Street, London, EC, at the date of publication of this book.

THE END

Other books by this author

Black Ivory

Red Rooney

The Coral Island

The Golden Dream

The Hot Swamp

The Island Queen

The Red Eric

Fast in the Ice

Sunk at Sea

The Battle and the Breeze

Chasing The Sun

R. M. Ballantyne

Choose from Thousands of 1stWorldLibrary Classics By

A. M. Barnard
Ada Leverson
Adolphus William Ward
Aesop
Agatha Christie
Alexander Aaronsohn
Alexander Kielland
Alexandre Dumas
Alfred Gatty
Alfred Ollivant
Alice Duer Miller
Alice Turner Curtis
Alice Dunbar
Allen Chapman
Alleyne Ireland
Ambrose Bierce
Amelia E. Barr
Amory H. Bradford
Andrew Lang
Andrew McFarland Davis
Andy Adams
Angela Brazil
Anna Alice Chapin
Anna Sewell
Annie Besant
Annie Hamilton Donnell
Annie Payson Call
Annie Roe Carr
Annonaymous
Anton Chekhov
Archibald Lee Fletcher
Arnold Bennett
Arthur C. Benson
Arthur Conan Doyle
Arthur M. Winfield
Arthur Ransome
Arthur Schnitzler
Arthur Train
Atticus
B.H. Baden-Powell
B. M. Bower
B. C. Chatterjee
Baroness Emmuska Orczy
Baroness Orczy
Basil King
Bayard Taylor
Ben Macomber
Bertha Muzzy Bower
Bjornstjerne Bjornson

Booth Tarkington
Boyd Cable
Bram Stoker
C. Collodi
C. E. Orr
C. M. Ingleby
Carolyn Wells
Catherine Parr Traill
Charles A. Eastman
Charles Amory Beach
Charles Dickens
Charles Dudley Warner
Charles Farrar Browne
Charles Ives
Charles Kingsley
Charles Klein
Charles Hanson Towne
Charles Lathrop Pack
Charles Romyn Dake
Charles Whibley
Charles Willing Beale
Charlotte M. Braeme
Charlotte M. Yonge
Charlotte Perkins Stetson
Clair W. Hayes
Clarence Day Jr.
Clarence E. Mulford
Clemence Housman
Confucius
Coningsby Dawson
Cornelis DeWitt Wilcox
Cyril Burleigh
D. H. Lawrence
Daniel Defoe
David Garnett
Dinah Craik
Don Carlos Janes
Donald Keyhoe
Dorothy Kilner
Dougan Clark
Douglas Fairbanks
E. Nesbit
E. P. Roe
E. Phillips Oppenheim
E. S. Brooks
Earl Barnes
Edgar Rice Burroughs
Edith Van Dyne
Edith Wharton

Edward Everett Hale
Edward J. O'Biren
Edward S. Ellis
Edwin L. Arnold
Eleanor Atkins
Eleanor Hallowell Abbott
Eliot Gregory
Elizabeth Gaskell
Elizabeth McCracken
Elizabeth Von Arnim
Ellem Key
Emerson Hough
Emilie F. Carlen
Emily Bronte
Emily Dickinson
Enid Bagnold
Enilor Macartney Lane
Erasmus W. Jones
Ernie Howard Pie
Ethel May Dell
Ethel Turner
Ethel Watts Mumford
Eugene Sue
Eugenie Foa
Eugene Wood
Eustace Hale Ball
Evelyn Everett-green
Everard Cotes
F. H. Cheley
F. J. Cross
F. Marion Crawford
Fannie E. Newberry
Federick Austin Ogg
Ferdinand Ossendowski
Fergus Hume
Florence A. Kilpatrick
Fremont B. Deering
Francis Bacon
Francis Darwin
Frances Hodgson Burnett
Frances Parkinson Keyes
Frank Gee Patchin
Frank Harris
Frank Jewett Mather
Frank L. Packard
Frank V. Webster
Frederic Stewart Isham
Frederick Trevor Hill
Frederick Winslow Taylor

Friedrich Kerst
Friedrich Nietzsche
Fyodor Dostoyevsky
G.A. Henty
G.K. Chesterton
Gabrielle E. Jackson
Garrett P. Serviss
Gaston Leroux
George A. Warren
George Ade
Geroge Bernard Shaw
George Cary Eggleston
George Durston
George Ebers
George Eliot
George Gissing
George MacDonald
George Meredith
George Orwell
George Sylvester Viereck
George Tucker
George W. Cable
George Wharton James
Gertrude Atherton
Gordon Casserly
Grace E. King
Grace Gallatin
Grace Greenwood
Grant Allen
Guillermo A. Sherwell
Gulielma Zollinger
Gustav Flaubert
H. A. Cody
H. B. Irving
H. C. Bailey
H. G. Wells
H. H. Munro
H. Irving Hancock
H. R. Naylor
H. Rider Haggard
H. W. C. Davis
Haldeman Julius
Hall Caine
Hamilton Wright Mabie
Hans Christian Andersen
Harold Avery
Harold McGrath
Harriet Beecher Stowe
Harry Castlemon
Harry Coghill
Harry Houidini

Hayden Carruth
Helent Hunt Jackson
Helen Nicolay
Hendrik Conscience
Hendy David Thoreau
Henri Barbusse
Henrik Ibsen
Henry Adams
Henry Ford
Henry Frost
Henry James
Henry Jones Ford
Henry Seton Merriman
Henry W Longfellow
Herbert A. Giles
Herbert Carter
Herbert N. Casson
Herman Hesse
Hildegard G. Frey
Homer
Honore De Balzac
Horace B. Day
Horace Walpole
Horatio Alger Jr.
Howard Pyle
Howard R. Garis
Hugh Lofting
Hugh Walpole
Humphry Ward
Ian Maclaren
Inez Haynes Gillmore
Irving Bacheller
Isabel Cecilia Williams
Isabel Hornibrook
Israel Abrahams
Ivan Turgenev
J. G.Austin
J. Henri Fabre
J. M. Barrie
J. M. Walsh
J. Macdonald Oxley
J. R. Miller
J. S. Fletcher
J. S. Knowles
J. Storer Clouston
J. W. Duffield
Jack London
Jacob Abbott
James Allen
James Andrews
James Baldwin

James Branch Cabell
James DeMille
James Joyce
James Lane Allen
James Lane Allen
James Oliver Curwood
James Oppenheim
James Otis
James R. Driscoll
Jane Abbott
Jane Austen
Jane L. Stewart
Janet Aldridge
Jens Peter Jacobsen
Jerome K. Jerome
Jessie Graham Flower
John Buchan
John Burroughs
John Cournos
John F. Kennedy
John Gay
John Glasworthy
John Habberton
John Joy Bell
John Kendrick Bangs
John Milton
John Philip Sousa
John Taintor Foote
Jonas Lauritz Idemil Lie
Jonathan Swift
Joseph A. Altsheler
Joseph Carey
Joseph Conrad
Joseph E. Badger Jr
Joseph Hergesheimer
Joseph Jacobs
Jules Vernes
Julian Hawthrone
Julie A Lippmann
Justin Huntly McCarthy
Kakuzo Okakura
Karle Wilson Baker
Kate Chopin
Kenneth Grahame
Kenneth McGaffey
Kate Langley Bosher
Kate Langley Bosher
Katherine Cecil Thurston
Katherine Stokes
L. A. Abbot
L. T. Meade

L. Frank Baum	Paul G. Tomlinson	T. S. Arthur
Latta Griswold	Paul Severing	The Princess Der Ling
Laura Dent Crane	Percy Brebner	Thomas A. Janvier
Laura Lee Hope	Percy Keese Fitzhugh	Thomas A Kempis
Laurence Housman	Peter B. Kyne	Thomas Anderton
Lawrence Beasley	Plato	Thomas Bailey Aldrich
Leo Tolstoy	Quincy Allen	Thomas Bulfinch
Leonid Andreyev	R. Derby Holmes	Thomas De Quincey
Lewis Carroll	R. L. Stevenson	Thomas Dixon
Lewis Sperry Chafer	R. S. Ball	Thomas H. Huxley
Lilian Bell	Rabindranath Tagore	Thomas Hardy
Lloyd Osbourne	Rahul Alvares	Thomas More
Louis Hughes	Ralph Bonehill	Thornton W. Burgess
Louis Joseph Vance	Ralph Henry Barbour	U. S. Grant
Louis Tracy	Ralph Victor	Upton Sinclair
Louisa May Alcott	Ralph Waldo Emmerson	Valentine Williams
Lucy Fitch Perkins	Rene Descartes	Various Authors
Lucy Maud Montgomery	Ray Cummings	Vaughan Kester
Luther Benson	Rex Beach	Victor Appleton
Lydia Miller Middleton	Rex E. Beach	Victor G. Durham
Lyndon Orr	Richard Harding Davis	Victoria Cross
M. Corvus	Richard Jefferies	Virginia Woolf
M. H. Adams	Richard Le Gallienne	Wadsworth Camp
Margaret E. Sangster	Robert Barr	Walter Camp
Margret Howth	Robert Frost	Walter Scott
Margaret Vandercook	Robert Gordon Anderson	Washington Irving
Margaret W. Hungerford	Robert L. Drake	Wilbur Lawton
Margret Penrose	Robert Lansing	Wilkie Collins
Maria Edgeworth	Robert Lynd	Willa Cather
Maria Thompson Daviess	Robert Michael Ballantyne	Willard F. Baker
Mariano Azuela	Robert W. Chambers	William Dean Howells
Marion Polk Angellotti	Rosa Nouchette Carey	William le Queux
Mark Overton	Rudyard Kipling	W. Makepeace Thackeray
Mark Twain	Saint Augustine	William W. Walter
Mary Austin	Samuel B. Allison	William Shakespeare
Mary Catherine Crowley	Samuel Hopkins Adams	Winston Churchill
Mary Cole	Sarah Bernhardt	Yei Theodora Ozaki
Mary Hastings Bradley	Sarah C. Hallowell	Yogi Ramacharaka
Mary Roberts Rinehart	Selma Lagerlof	Young E. Allison
Mary Rowlandson	Sherwood Anderson	Zane Grey
M. Wollstonecraft Shelley	Sigmund Freud	
Maud Lindsay	Standish O'Grady	
Max Beerbohm	Stanley Weyman	
Myra Kelly	Stella Benson	
Nathaniel Hawthrone	Stella M. Francis	
Nicolo Machiavelli	Stephen Crane	
O. F. Walton	Stewart Edward White	
Oscar Wilde	Stijn Streuvels	
Owen Johnson	Swami Abhedananda	
P.G. Wodehouse	Swami Parmananda	
Paul and Mabel Thorne	T. S. Ackland